WAR MEMOIR OF A HAMBURG FAMILY

SOUND
AND
FURY

PETER
BARTH

The Book Guild Ltd

First published in Great Britain in 2022 by
The Book Guild Ltd
Unit E2 Airfield Business Park,
Harrison Road, Market Harborough,
Leicestershire. LE16 7UL
Freephone: 0800 999 2982
www.bookguild.co.uk
Email: info@bookguild.co.uk
Twitter: @bookguild

Typeset in 12pt Adobe Jenson Pro

Printed on FSC accredited paper
Printed and bound in Great Britain by 4edge Limited

ISBN 978 1914471 384

British Library Cataloguing in Publication Data.
A catalogue record for this book is available from the British Library.

SOUND
AND
FURY

To my mother Dolly, who looked after my sister Annemarie and me, very often on her own, with determination and love during the very difficult war years in Germany and later when we came to England. Through her love and selfless care, she gave us a happy and secure childhood.

Contents

Introduction

I come from a family with relatives from England, Germany and Denmark (Family Tree, pxiii) My mother Dolly was born and brought up in London. On a visit to Hamburg shortly before the Second World War, she met and married my German father, Maximilian Barth. My sister Annemarie and I were both born in Hamburg and spent the Second World War years in Germany. After the bombing and destruction of Hamburg in July 1943, we were scattered for the remaining years of the war. Most of the family managed to return to Hamburg after the war. In 1946, our mother Dolly returned to England, taking us two children.

During our growing up in England we heard many stories from our mother about our life in Germany during the war and what happened to our family. The stories of our family's history were interesting because of my mother's unusual circumstances: she was living in a country which was at war with the country of her birth, where most of her family were still living. She encountered no hostility in Germany, but to our family, it was a civil war. These stories seemed worth preserving.

At first I based the stories on a number of cassette recordings I had made of conversations with my mother and sister sitting round the tea table. When we visited my cousin Werner Hamelmann and his wife Henny in Fischen, Bavaria (in 2002 and 2005), I took the opportunity to record their stories too. Werner was a great raconteur and had many amazing tales to tell about his life in the army during the war years. It gave us an insight into the Second World War from the viewpoint of a young German soldier, just out of school, still in his teens. There were also my own memories, some direct and some of conversations after the war with family members. I had a few letters, documents and photographs of family events that helped me fill some of the gaps of our time in Germany. However, I do regret that when we first went back to Hamburg after the war in 1954 to visit our families there, instead of taking pictures of the vast bombed-out city areas, including where we used to live, I photographed animals in Hagenbeck's wonderful zoo instead. A great opportunity missed! I was 13 and found the zoo animals much more appealing than the acres of bombed-out houses.

Werner, my German cousin, was a great letter writer, great in both senses. He asked his mother, my aunt Trudel, to keep his letters safe so that they could become a memoir of his war years in Russia, Denmark, Norway, France etc. And so they proved to be. A few months after starting to write, I discovered that Achim Hammelmann, my cousin Werner's eldest son, his wife Uta and Werner's wife, Henny, had curated and digitized a collection of over 450 letters that the family had collected during the war years. Achim has published over half of these letters as a neobooks.com *eBook*, "Ich bin jetzt Soldat, 1942-46, das Leben einer Familie aus Hamburg in 280 Briefen". Achim and Uta kindly sent me the full collection of the "Feldpost" letters. They are all in German so I had to polish up and augment my vocabulary with a glossary of military and other less familiar words and expressions. Mostly, I have not produced word for word translations of these letters: I shortened the narrative to keep the momentum of the events described. Anyone wanting to read the full originals can refer to Achim's e-book, using the dates I have put in brackets as Feldpost cross references.

Another very important source of material came from Klaus Melchers, grandson of my aunt Else Koschel, Trudel's sister. Klaus sent me large collections of digitized family photos, documents and diaries as well as his memories via long internet conversations. He patiently filled the gaps in my knowledge and corrected many of my misunderstandings of past events. Using these sources I have been able to piece together some of the stories of what happened to my extended family during the war years. Klaus explained the spelling of the Hamelmann/ Hammelmann name. Adam changed his name by deed-poll from Hammelmann to Hamelmann. Apparently, it cost him a lot of money but he thought it worthwhile because in German "Hammel" means "mutton", but pejoratively, it means "ass" or "donkey". Hammelmann is a fairly common German name, Hamelmann is rare. Werner's sons decided to return to the original spelling of Hammelmann.

Before the war, after my mother's marriage, the Barths, the Hamelmanns and the Koschels all lived near each other in the beautiful Uhlenhorst district on the eastern shore of Hamburg's large Alster Lake. Then in July 1943, three massive bombing raids by the RAF, called Operation Gomorrah, destroyed most of Hamburg, Germany's second largest city. Tens of thousands of people were killed but fortunately, our families all survived. We were among the 1.2 million people evacuated from Hamburg after the second Gomorrah bombing raid. This became our families' diaspora.

My cousin Werner Hamelmann was already in the Wehrmacht (army). He was sent back to Russia by train to rejoin his company. His brother Walter, who was only 16, had to remain in Hamburg on flak and fire-fighting duties. Their mother Trudel went to stay with relatives of her husband in the Pfalz region. My grandfather (Opa) Max joined Trudel soon afterwards. Trudel's husband, Adam Hamelmann was the chief steward on a luxury cruise liner, the Cap Arcona. She had been requisitioned in 1940 by the Kriegsmarine (German Navy) and berthed in the Bay of Gdynia in the Baltic Sea. He had to return to his ship.

Else and Richard Koschel (my aunt and uncle) and their daughter Rosi also fled from Hamburg and returned to their second home in Krakau (in German-occupied Poland). Their son Edgar, was recruited into the Luftwaffe and was posted to France.

My mother Dolly, sister Annemarie and I were also evacuated from Hamburg after the bombing. For a year we were refugees in a small town in Bavaria. My father, Maximilian was in the army in occupied France but, soon after Gomorrah, he was also sent to the Russian front, just a month after Werner got there. Both men came back badly wounded, my father being half-starved as well. Werner was posted to Norway and later to Normandy after the Allied invasion. Maximilian was put on fire duties in Hamburg. My mother Dolly, Annemarie and I moved from Bavaria to a farm house in a village called Oldendorf, on Lüneburg Heath. It was just 10 km away from Bergen-Belsen, a village of no obvious significance to us then.

Towards the end of the war, our families returned to Hamburg, our home city, though not all of us had survived. Adam Hamelmann was on the Cap Arcona ferrying refugees and wounded soldiers to Denmark and west Germany. The Koschels took almost a year to get back from Krakau, narrowly missing the bombing of Dresden and other dangers. Some of the experiences and tragedies in the lives we led during those war years are related in this book.

Barth - Mikkelsen Family

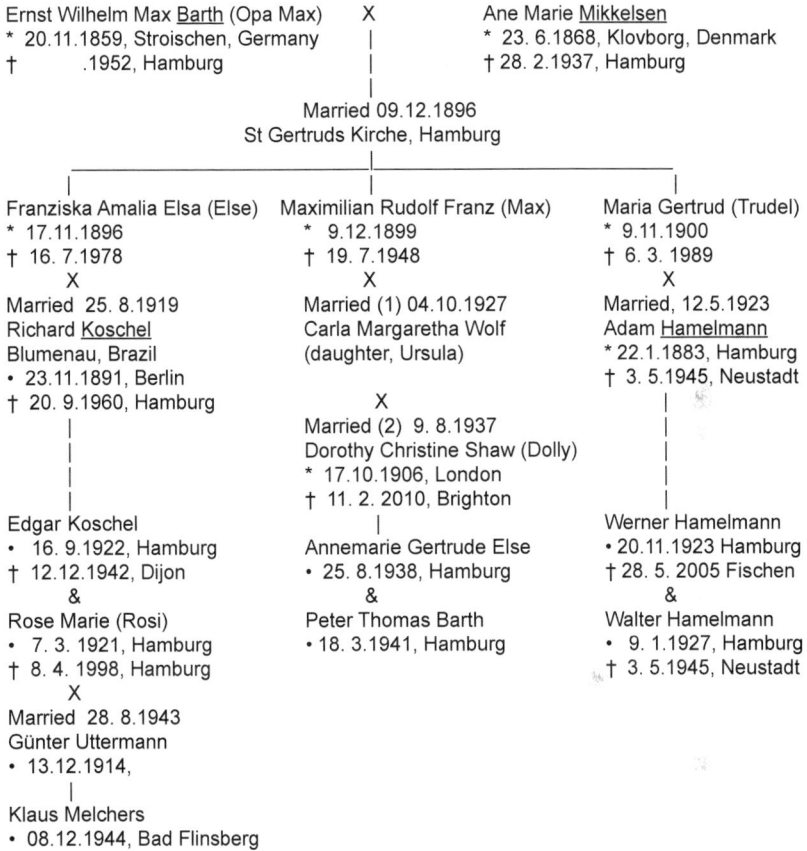

Ernst Wilhelm Max <u>Barth</u> (Opa Max)	X	Ane Marie <u>Mikkelsen</u>
* 20.11.1859, Stroischen, Germany		* 23. 6.1868, Klovborg, Denmark
† .1952, Hamburg		† 28. 2.1937, Hamburg

Married 09.12.1896
St Gertruds Kirche, Hamburg

Franziska Amalia Elsa (Else)	Maximilian Rudolf Franz (Max)	Maria Gertrud (Trudel)
* 17.11.1896	* 9.12.1899	* 9.11.1900
† 16. 7.1978	† 19. 7.1948	† 6. 3. 1989
X	X	X
Married 25. 8.1919	Married (1) 04.10.1927	Married, 12.5.1923
Richard <u>Koschel</u>	Carla Margaretha Wolf	Adam <u>Hamelmann</u>
Blumenau, Brazil	(daughter, Ursula)	* 22.1.1883, Hamburg
• 23.11.1891, Berlin	X	† 3. 5.1945, Neustadt
† 20. 9.1960, Hamburg	Married (2) 9. 8.1937	
	Dorothy Christine Shaw (Dolly)	
	* 17.10.1906, London	
	† 11. 2. 2010, Brighton	
Edgar Koschel		Werner Hamelmann
• 16. 9.1922, Hamburg	Annemarie Gertrude Else	• 20.11.1923 Hamburg
† 12.12.1942, Dijon	• 25. 8.1938, Hamburg	† 28. 5. 2005 Fischen
&	&	&
Rose Marie (Rosi)	Peter Thomas Barth	Walter Hamelmann
• 7. 3. 1921, Hamburg	• 18. 3.1941, Hamburg	• 9. 1.1927, Hamburg
† 8. 4. 1998, Hamburg		† 3. 5.1945, Neustadt
X		
Married 28. 8.1943		
Günter Uttermann		
• 13.12.1914,		

Klaus Melchers
• 08.12.1944, Bad Flinsberg

Sühr - Schäfer Family

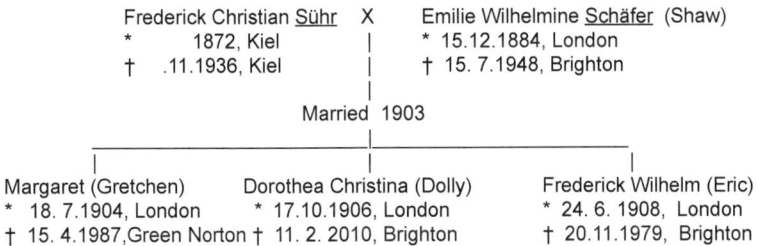

Frederick Christian <u>Sühr</u>	X	Emilie Wilhelmine <u>Schäfer</u> (Shaw)
* 1872, Kiel		* 15.12.1884, London
† .11.1936, Kiel		† 15. 7.1948, Brighton

Married 1903

Margaret (Gretchen)	Dorothea Christina (Dolly)	Frederick Wilhelm (Eric)
* 18. 7.1904, London	* 17.10.1906, London	* 24. 6. 1908, London
† 15. 4.1987,Green Norton	† 11. 2. 2010, Brighton	† 20.11.1979, Brighton

Chapter One

My Families: an Anglo-Saxon Alliance

My mother, christened Dorothea Christine Sühr, was born in London, Islington on the 17th of October 1906, not far from the famous "Angel, Islington", a historic landmark and Inn. It was said that some part of a real Angel entered into her at birth, accounting for her generous, kind and loving nature. She was usually called Dolly. Her mother, Emilie Wilhelmine Schäfer was born in London in 1884 but her family lived in Kiel, Germany. At that time many Germans were drawn to London, the centre of the British Empire, to seek work in what was then the richest city in Europe. There was a substantial flow of people back and forth across the North Sea at that time. Emilie often visited her family in Kiel. It was on one of these trips that she met her future husband, Frederick Sühr. He was born in 1872, the eldest of 12 children.

Frederick came to London and found a job as a waiter. He worked his way up the ladder and became head wine waiter (sommelier) at the famous and exclusive Trocadero Restaurant in London's West End. It was the sort of restaurant where full evening dress was worn by the diners. Frederick and Emilie were married in 1903 in London. His income by that time must have been substantial because they could afford to live in a large house: No.13 Myddelton Square. Frederick and Emilie took in "paying guests" or lodgers as we would call them now. In the 1911 census, the house was occupied by the family, four lodgers and a maid. It was listed as having 10 rooms.

Between 1904 and 1908 Emilie gave birth to three children, Margaret (Gretchen), Dorothy (my mother, Dolly) and Frederick (Eric). For much of the year, all three children slept in a small summer house in the garden, leaving more room in the house for the "guests". In the centre of Myddelton Square is a very fine church surrounded by gardens. The children used to play there as well as in their own garden. Sometimes, if they trod on the flower beds of the church garden, the gardener chased them off, shouting and waving his broom.

When the First World War broke out, Frederick Sühr was interned on the Isle of Man as an "enemy alien". This occurred

Sühr Family ca 1910: Frederick, Eric, Dolly,
Emilie and Gretchen (plus the maid standing behind).

despite the fact that he was resident and employed in England. He was also married to a British wife and was the father of three childen, all born in London, all British citizens. It is not clear why he was interned. They speculated it was because he had failed to seek British citizenship during his time in England. At the end of the war, when he was released, Emilie divorced him although, according to my mother, he had been a very good husband and father to his children. It may have been because Germans were treated with such virulent hatred and contempt in England after the war that Emilie was not willing to face it, she would hide her German connections. However, there is another theory, based only on rumour: that Frederick had got the maid pregnant and Emilie unforgivingly denounced him to the authorities. Whatever the reason, he was deported to Germany and returned to his home city of Kiel.

Shortly after this, the family in London anglicized their surname to "Shaw" by deed-poll. Emilie chose Shaw perhaps because of some similarity to her maiden name, Schäfer but more likely because she was very fond of G.B.Shaw's plays. How she managed financially after the divorce is not clear. The lodgers obviously provided some of her income. However, she was closely linked to the local church and, it seems, she was to some extent supported by the "League for Distressed Gentlefolk".

The Shaw family seemed to live pretty well. Emilie regularly took her children to the theatre, ballet, concerts, opera and art galleries as well as passing on her love of books, Dickens in particular. She was artistic, producing some lovely framed drawings and paintings. She painted birthday cards with little poems inside, one of which I still have. However, my mother, Dolly, suffered from rickets when she was a girl. This is caused by a lack of vitamin D which is found in oil and fatty foods. It is also synthesized in the skin when exposed to sunlight. Emilie may have served their cultural needs but neglected their physical welfare. The children noted that their mother always had the best foods, including butter and cheese, while they got the basic cheap stuff ("bread and scrape"). There were other things in her life that showed she was very self-centred and selfish with respect to her children. Despite this, all three grew up as generous, warm-hearted, amusing and loving people.

Saxony and Schleswig

My father, Maximilian Rudolf Franz Barth, was born in Hamburg on 9 December 1899, just before the turn of the century and just a year after the death of Otto von Bismarck. His father, also known as Max, was born Ernst Wilhelm Max Barth on 20 November 1859, in a small village called Stroischen, about 8 km west of Meissen. Stroischen consisted of five farm houses with various barns clustered around a duck pond in the middle of the village. It looks much the same now. Grandfather Max, or Opa Max as he was known later, was born before the unification of Germany. In 1871, Otto von Bismarck, Minister President of Prussia, created the German Empire which consisted of a federation of 26 Kingdoms, Grand Duchies, Duchies, Principalities, Free and Hanseatic Cities and Imperial Territories. Stroischen was in the Kingdom of Saxony.

Just three years after German Unification, Max was apprenticed to a blacksmith and gained his qualifying certificate on 30 May 1877 in Meissen. Around this time, Bismarck was commonly depicted as the strong blacksmith forging the sword of German Unity. He declared that the future unity of the German people would be decided not by speeches but by "iron and blood." He was therefore nicknamed "the Iron Chancellor". Bismarck was a member of the rich land-owning aristocracy, the Junckers, and was clearly not thought of as a manual worker: the blacksmith label was purely metaphorical. It is also worth noting that, not far west of Meissen, was the ancient Saxon Duchy of Saxe-Coburg and Gotha which had a lucrative industry in this era: exporting aristocracy, including Prince Albert to Great Britain.

Some time after he qualified as a blacksmith, Max packed his bags and went off to Hamburg to seek a new life. He probably went by steamboat from Meissen along the river Elbe which links the two cities. In Hamburg he continued his education and learnt the locksmith's trade. Bismarck's new German Empire had a strong strain of Prussian militarism. In the new united Germany, all fit young men had to undergo training in the armed forces. Max's military record shows that he passed his training on 20 Sept 1883, at the age of 23, in Nuremberg. He was given a first class score for shooting and issued with "a uniform, trousers, underpants, neckband, shirt and a pair of boots". On 1st April 1889 he used his train pass to travel from Nuremberg back to Hamburg.

One of the big issues Bismarck needed to resolve before bringing about the unification of Germany was the Schleswig-Holstein question. The Duchies of Schleswig and Holstein were at the centre of a complicated dispute between Denmark and Germany which had been going on for hundreds of years. For most of that time they were independent Duchies (ruled by dukes). However in 1863, King Christian IX of Denmark decided, unilaterally, to incorporate the Duchy of Schleswig fully into Denmark. This violated the existing "London Protocol" and led to the Second Schleswig War of 1864. Combined Prussian and Austrian troops crossed the Eider river, the border between Holstein and Schleswig, and rapidly won control. A peace treaty was signed whereby the border between Denmark and Germany was redrawn through the middle of Schleswig, just north of Flensburg. The everyday language used by the majority of the inhabitants of both Duchies was German, but there was a majority of Danish speakers in the northern half of Schleswig. The Duchies were thus absorbed into Denmark and Germany, roughly along the language border. Later plebiscites confirmed that this division was popular with the majority of the inhabitants and so the dispute was finally laid to rest.

Fortunately, the people of this region continued to migrate across the border or I would not be here. One such person was my grandmother Ane Marie Mikkelsen. She was born on 23 June 1868 in Klovborg, Flårits Mark, Denmark, just four years after the second Schleswig War. Her father, Jens Mikkelsen, was first married to Johanne Pedersen who gave birth to three children. When she died, aged only 25, he married her sister, Anne Kirstine Pedersen. They then produced a further ten children (not including a stillborn son) born regularly over the course of twenty years or so. Ane Marie's younger sister, Johanne Mikkelsen, married Jørgen Hroar Fog. She gave birth to a son called Asbjørn Fog who grew up to be a priest and a missionary in Nigeria. My cousin Werner knew him and met him in 1944 as he was passing through Aarhus on his way to Norway (Chapter 10).

When Ane Marie was in her twenties, she travelled south to Hamburg to look for work (and perhaps to get out of an overcrowded house). She found a job in a fish shop in Zimmerstraße the street in which Max Barth, the locksmith, lived. They met there, perhaps discussing the price of herrings on the slab. She was an Angle and he was a Saxon. They got to know each other and formed a fruitful Anglo-Saxon Alliance.

Max Barth and Ane Marie Mikkelsen were married on 5 December 1896 in the nearby Lutheran

Ane Marie and Max Barth, marriage 1896.

Church of St Gertrud. This seems to have been socially necessary as their first child, Franziska Amalia Elsa, had already been born three weeks earlier, on 17 November 1896. She was known to everybody as Else. Three years later, on 9 December 1899, Ane Marie gave birth to a second child, a son, Maximilian Rudolf Franz Barth, my father. And just a year after that, on 9 November 1900, a second daughter was born, Maria Gertrud Barth, known as Trudel. The locksmith's trade and the fish shop must have been quite lucrative because they lived in a fine spacious apartment in Zimmerstraße 38, which was in the beautiful Uhlenhorst district of Hamburg. After some time, Ane Marie took over the running of the fish shop. On the 29th April 1904, Max Barth was granted, via a magnificent certificate, "Citizenship of the Free and Hanseatic City of Hamburg". Perhaps this came in recognition of his contributions to the locksmith's art or for his contribution to the population with the birth of their three lovely children, Else, Maximilian and Trudel. (Actually, it depended only on a trouble-free period of residency.)

Barth Family 1914: Mother Ane Marie,
Gertrud, Father Max, Maximilian, Else.

The three children grew up and went to school in Hamburg. At that time there was a strong connection between Germany and South America, which was seen as their land of opportunity, just as the Pilgrim Fathers from England had seen North America as their New Jerusalem. In her late teens, Else went to Brazil as an au pair. This story is continued in Chapter 7, The Koschels in Krakau, where you will also learn how Trudel met *her* future husband, Adam, on the cruise ship Cap Arcona.

Barth Family 1925: Ane Marie, Opa Max, Else,
Maximilian, children in front: Edgar and Rosi.

Chapter Two

The Meeting and Marriage of Max and Dolly

My mother, Dolly, grew up in London but kept in touch with her deported father, Frederick Sühr, who was living in his home city of Kiel. In 1922, when she was 16, Dolly went to stay with him for 9 months. She loved her father dearly and went to see him every summer. Frederick loved his children and was very caring and generous to Dolly when she was with him in Germany. During her long visit she received a telegram from her mother, Emilie, saying that she was very ill, possibly dying, and needed Dolly to return to London at once. So she went back only to find that there was absolutely nothing wrong with her selfish mother: she just wanted Dolly back home to cook, clean and look after her.

Emilie was full of religious trappings but was actually uncaring of and selfish to all three of her children. Gretchen had a strong personality and did not put up with it for long. She left home in her late teens and went to live with her Aunty Marie (Emilie's sister) who was a very colourful character. They got on well together: Gretchen had a more exciting and fuller life with her aunt. Eric was farmed out for a while to a foster mother, a sweet old lady, living in Harborne, Birmingham (I visited her in 1964). There was even a plan mooted to have him adopted by an Australian man who would have taken Eric back to his home "Down-under". Emilie hung onto Dolly only because of her nursing skills and willingness to work hard and selflessly.

Dolly trained to be a nurse at St Bartholomew's Hospital in London and then worked for five years as a ward nurse. After that she was employed in a fever hospital. Throughout this time she kept in touch with her father and visited him in Germany every summer, generally for about a month. Frederick Sühr was remarried, to a woman called Rosa, who was also very fond of Dolly. Because of the warm and loving atmosphere, Dolly always enjoyed her visits to her father.

After his deportation to Germany, Frederick settled in his home city of Kiel. He looked for opportunities in the business he knew best: catering. Not far from Kiel, on the west coast of the peninsular, is a beautiful town called Heide, built in the 15th Century. (It claims to have the largest open market square in Germany.) Frederick took a lease on the elegant restaurant adjacent to the Heide Racecourse which was very famous: it was the "Aintree" of its day in Germany and attracted large crowds on race days. Frederick and Rosa lived in rooms at the back of the restaurant. Dolly stayed with them there during her visits. Rosa helped with the cooking and running of the restaurant along with other staff. On race days they had a method of making "instant coffee" which intrigued Dolly. They prepared a large jug of very strong coffee at the end of the evening. The following day when a coffee was ordered, they would pour a measure of this concentrate into a cup and then add boiling water. It was apparently very good and they could serve a lot of people quickly that way.

The restaurant had a dance-floor. During race weeks they provided music and dancing evenings. Dolly usually went to the dances and enjoyed the social life. She met a young man there, called Martin, who was a baker supplying her father's restaurant.

He became her boyfriend for a while and took her out on his motorbike to see the countryside and places around Heide. As well as horse racing, the race syndicate organized car or motorbike racing events using a raised sloping track around the edge of the racecourse. This attracted large crowds. Frederick's restaurant and dance-hall were very popular and successful for many years. This, in turn, attracted the unwelcome attention of Nazi Stormtroopers who were always looking for money they could loot (for the good of the Party and the Reich of course!). It was rumoured that the Nazis were snooping around, so Frederick and Rosa cleared the till and hid their money and a few valuables. They were successful in evading the Nazis.

In the mid 1930s, due to the depression and hyper-inflation in Germany, the racecourse syndicate went bankrupt. This hit Frederick and Rosa hard: without the race-goers the business was not viable, they had to close it. They started looking for a new venue in Heide or Kiel. They couldn't find anywhere suitable after many months so they went to the much larger city of Hamburg to look for a pub or restaurant. They found a small pub at the corner of Zimmerstraße in the Uhlenhorst district of Hamburg. They thought they could run it profitably, so Frederick rented it. It was much smaller than their lovely restaurant in Heide, of course, but the economy in Germany was struggling at that time and this was the best they could do. Perhaps because of the economic difficulties, Rosa started drinking more heavily. To cover it up, and not hit the profits, she used to persuade customers to buy her drinks. She also started an affair with a young man behind Frederick's back, much to Dolly's disgust.

In the summer of 1936, Dolly visited her father in Hamburg. It was there in that pub that she first met Maximilian Barth. He lived in Zimmerstraße, this was his local. She found him "quite fascinating, he was amusing, intelligent and handsome". He also had a fine singing voice, which she heard in the pub on many jolly occasions. So they got to know each other that summer.

As usual, after her visits, Dolly went back to London to her job in the hospital. She told her family all about Maximilian. Her mother was not pleased with her absences in Germany because she still wanted Dolly to look after her all the time as an unpaid nurse and cook. In October 1936, Dolly's father Frederick fell ill and she got permission from her hospital matron to go and visit him. She found him in a very overcrowded ward in a hospital in Kiel. He was upset about Rosa's drinking and philandering with the young man. Dolly was only given a short leave of absence from her hospital and had to return to London. Three weeks after getting back home, Frederick Sühr died. Dolly and Eric went to Kiel for the funeral but their mother, Emilie, didn't go with them. She was not willing to make the effort, to show respect for the father of their three children, even though she may have ceased to love him. Soon after Frederick's death, Rosa married the young man with whom she had been having an affair.

In February of the following year 1937, Maximilian's mother, Ane Marie Barth, died after suffering a stroke. Max wrote to Dolly asking her to come to Hamburg and marry him. Dolly told the matron at the hospital about her plans to get married. The matron asked if she would be willing to come back to the hospital after the wedding as they were keen to keep her. Dolly explained that they had other plans. They wanted to live in Hamburg because most of Maximilian's family lived there and he had a well-paid job as an accountant in the city. It also gave her an escape from her domineering mother in London.

This would be Max's second marriage. His first marriage was to Carla Margaretha Minna Wolf, on the 4 October 1927 in Hamburg. They moved to Bolivia where Max had an export/import business with Hamburg. Carla gave birth to a daughter called Ursula and they continued to live in Bolivia. For unknown reasons the marriage broke up and they were divorced in January 1934. Carla and Ursula remained in Bolivia for many years after that and moved to Munich after the war. Dolly never got to meet them. She didn't seem to know much about Max's previous marriage to Carla or why it had broken up.

Dolly arrived in Hamburg's Hauptbahnhof (main station) in early July 1937. Max was there to meet her. She had brought her portable gramophone and collection of records. When she went through customs at the German border, they looked carefully at all the records to make sure that they conformed to the strict Nazi cultural rules (no "degenerate" black or Jewish music). In order to get married, Dolly had to undergo scrutiny of her family documents in the following weeks to see if she also conformed to the strict Nazi Aryan heredity rules. She passed both tests. Max and Dolly got married in a Register Office in Hamburg on the 9th of August 1937 with Opa Max and his brother, Robert Barth, as witnesses.

Wedding of Dolly and Maximilian 1937:
Robert, Dolly, Maximilian and Max Barth.

They were married in rather odd circumstances. Although Zimmerstraße seemed to be almost entirely populated by his family, Max did not go out of his way to introduce them all to his new bride. He was not very popular with the rest of the family at this time, perhaps partly because of the divorce but certainly because he was spending too much time in the local pubs. So Max and Dolly had rather few guests at their wedding. They started married life just round the corner from Zimmerstraße in a small flat in Stormsweg, a short street which led down to a ship canal.

Eric Shaw, Dolly's brother, came over from London for the wedding. He stayed for a few days in their small flat but had to sleep on the sofa. After the wedding, the happy couple, Eric and a few guests met in the flat for the wedding reception, which, knowing my father, probably consisted of more drink than food. There was a knock at the door and a young lad presented my mother with a large bouquet of flowers. Thinking he was a delivery boy, she went off to find her purse and gave him a tip. However, it turned out he was Edgar Koschel, son of Else, Max's sister, who lived just across the street in Zimmerstraße. Max had not introduced them to Dolly. Edgar was perhaps too taken aback to say who he was. Later on when Dolly got to know Else, they became good friends. She was very helpful when my mother gave birth to her first baby a year later. Trudel hung back a bit at first but when she got to know Dolly better, she was also warm and friendly, often inviting her round for coffee and cakes.

Eric Shaw stayed in Hamburg for a few days after the wedding. Just a walk down Zimmerstraße and then Karlstraße, leads one to the Alster. Right there on the shore, overlooking the great lake, was the magnificent and famous Uhlenhorster Fährhaus. It had a restaurant, coffee rooms, beer hall and large music and dance rooms. Some of it was open-air so that you could eat and drink while looking across the Alster. It also had boating facilities where canoes for paddling around the lake were for hire. The weather was very fine that August, Eric was

Eric Sühr (Shaw) on the Alster, 1937.

enjoying himself so he stayed on for a few days, spending time at the Fährhaus. On one occasion he met a young man about the same age as himself called Karl-Heinz Tschöpe. Over some beers and a couple of sessions of canoeing they got to know each other. After the war Eric looked him up again and discovered that Karl-Heinz was back in Hamburg. He had married a bright and lively girl called Annie who had the most infectious laugh you ever heard. She had given birth to a son called Gerd who was two years younger than me. Towards the end of the war Karl-Heinz managed to get back to Hamburg from the Balkans via Austria, mostly on foot, but with a few lifts in lorries. He had been shot in the stomach in Russia and had to undergo an operation without anaesthetic. He was left with a long scar across his stomach and suffered permanent digestive disorders. After the war, our two families became life-long friends. But that's another story.

The Stormsweg flat overlooked the Feen Canal which was a wide ship canal connecting to the Alster via the Feenteich, a small lake. The flat was very small: just one bedroom, a sitting room and a kitchen. There was no bathroom as such, just a washbasin and toilet off the hall. There were local public baths nearby for the weekly scrub but my mother complained that they were very mean with the water: the bath was filled to a low level and that was all you got, no arguments! In the summer, a soap-down and dip in the canal was quite popular. My house-proud mother set about making the flat spick and span. It had beautiful pitch-pine floorboards. She got down on her knees, scouring and polishing them in true German fashion, until they gleamed. The curtains looked rather grubby so she washed them but they were so old, they fell to pieces in the wash. The sitting room had a lovely rug carpet which she also washed and then hung up to dry on the railing of the balcony overlooking the canal. A while later she noticed the rug had gone: the wind had blown it into the canal. With the help of a neighbour who had a long boat hook, they managed to rescue it before it floated away or sank. She was often teased about this later. However when she had dried the rug and put it back in place again, she was very pleased because the colours were so much brighter than before. Eric used to pee from the balcony into the canal if he was caught short in the night.

Maximilian and Dolly did not have to live very long in that small flat. Max's mother, Ane Marie, had died in February 1937, six months before Max and Dolly's marriage. During that time Opa Max lived on his own in his spacious apartment in Zimmerstraße 38. He was a kind, gentle and thoughtful man. He didn't need that much room, so he passed it on to Max and Dolly shortly after their marriage. Instead, he moved in with his daughter Trudel, her husband Adam Hamelmann and their boys, Werner and Walter, in Uhlenhorster Weg. As Adam was away at sea most of the time, it suited them all to have another man helping around the house. Opa would otherwise be living all alone. When the bombing of Hamburg started, he proved himself to be useful and brave (next chapter).

Chapter Three

Life in Hamburg, 1938 – 1942

The hiatus before the cataclysm: Hamburg
resurgam
Hamburg!

A year after their marriage, on 25 August 1938, Dolly gave birth to a girl, my sister, Annemarie Gertrude Else Barth, named after Max's mother and his two sisters. Else helped Dolly look after the baby and kept her company. Before the war, they had a happy life in Hamburg. Else, Dolly and little Annemarie often visited Hamburg's large and beautiful Stadt Park. It has fields and woods where they roamed. There are also meadows, flower gardens, sports facilities and cafes where they relaxed and talked over cups of coffee. The younger children have play areas and a paddling pool which was very popular in the summer.

Dolly also took Annemarie in the pram to the Alster Lake which was a pleasant walk down Zimmerstraße. There are green parks all round the lake with cafes and beer gardens. The Alsterdampfers (steam boats) run a public transport system

Annemarie and
Dolly Barth, 1938.

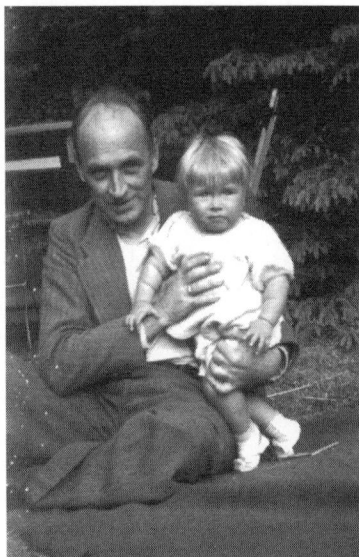

Maximilian and
Annemarie Barth, 1938.

across and around the lake. A boat ride to Jungfernstieg takes you to the centre of Hamburg, a beautiful and relaxing way to get there. All the big shops, Town Hall and other public buildings were there. Another pleasant day out was a trip by train (S-Bahn) to Blankenese a "seaside" village on the sandy north bank of the Elbe, downstream from Hamburg. It has beautiful villas and all the facilities of a seaside town including large sandy beaches.

The family also made trips to the seaside on the Baltic In the summer. Their favourite resort was Grömitz in the Bay of Lübeck. They stayed in a hotel or pension for a few days, taking walks along the promenade, eating ice creams, making sand castles and swimming in the sea. The beach had large wicker chairs to sit in which were typical of the bay resorts. They were useful to get out of the occasional wind and enjoy the sunshine. Another favourite place was Lüneburg Heath where they could take a picnic and then wander in the beautiful countryside, pick flowers, blackberries and mushrooms. They also visited some of the very picturesque ancient villages on the Heath, such as Undeloh and Wilsede.

When the honeymoon period was over, not everything was fine, however. Max continued to spend too much time in the pub. He enjoyed the atmosphere of lively chat and laughter and sometimes singing. However, he also drank too much. Dolly was left at home looking after her baby, Annemarie. Max would often came home late and drunk with all his money gone. She took to going to his office on Friday paydays and collecting his salary directly so that she could pay bills and feed the family. Sometimes he managed to evade her and did not come back until he had spent it all on alcohol. When he was in the army, money would come in regularly from the Wehrmacht, directly to Dolly, so she no longer had that worry.

Maximilian's behaviour was not new, however. Before their marriage, some time in the mid 1930s, Max was on a ship returning to Hamburg from Bolivia. He sent a telegram to Adam, his brother-in-law on the Cap Arcona, asking for a loan, which he promised to repay when they got to Hamburg. Adam duly wired him the money. When Max's ship docked in Hamburg, his sister Trudel and Opa Max were there, waiting to greet him. However, instead of coming down the main gang-plank with all the other passengers, he went to the stern of the ship where the stores were being loaded and sneeked down the service gang-plank. He disappeared into one of the many bars in the St Pauli docks area and turned up at home a couple of days later when all the money was gone.

*

On the 3rd of September 1939, the British Prime Minister, Neville Chamberlain declared war on Nazi Germany following the invasion of Poland two days earlier by Nazi storm-troopers. This broke the Munich Agreement between Germany, Britain,

France and Italy that had been forged with Hitler in 1938. It has usually been regarded since as a failed policy of "appeasement" of a dictator who had absolutely no intention of keeping to the terms of the Agreement. Dolly's mother Emilia (my grandmother) happened to be visiting her relatives in Berlin in August 1939. She could hear the drums of war beating. Emilia quickly made travel plans and returned home to London. She remembered the horrors of the First World War. As a British citizen she may well have been interned (as an enemy alien) if she had stayed in Germany after the declaration of war.

Life in Hamburg did not seem to change much after the declaration but the Nazis were continuing to build their war machine. Maximilian had been conscripted into the Wehrmacht in the last year of the First World War when he was 18. He hated it, he hated war altogether. He was called up again in WW2 when he was 41. He tried very hard to get out of it but didn't succeed. At the time he was running a firm in Hamburg called Heitmann's which dealt in wine, liqueurs and spirits. The owner had become seriously ill and had persuaded Max to take over the management. (Thoughts of a fox in charge of a hen-house come to mind.) However, Max could hardly claim he was doing important war-work and so he was conscripted into the Wehrmacht. He was sent to a barracks, probably the nearby Lüneburg Camp, for military training – in marching and shooting.

Very soon after this, In March 1941, my mother was undergoing her second pregnancy in the nearby Elise Averdieck hospital in Finkenau. Air-raid alarms suddenly went off and everyone had to go down into the cellars. The RAF made a significant bombing raid on Hamburg on the night of 12/13 March which killed a reported 51 people. Fortunately, our district of Uhlenhorst was not touched. Dolly gave birth to me a few days later, very soon after another air-raid warning, which luckily did not presage an actual attack. Throughout those years, the RAF continued to bomb Hamburg at irregular intervals. My mother, who was born in London and had most of her family still there, was teased as to why she didn't pick up the phone and tell her brother Eric to get these b***** air raids stopped!

My father proposed that I should be named Maximilian like himself and his father before him. (Our son's middle name is Maximilian.) However, my mother was not keen and named me Peter instead, partly because she liked it and partly because her mother Emilie, had taken to calling herself "Peta" among her arty friends. This could be a harking back to her mother's maiden name, Petersen, or a reference to the very popular book "Peter Pan" by J M Barrie. My middle name, Thomas, comes from the German nickname for British soldiers: "Tommys".

In June 1941, as part of the German occupation of France, my father was sent to a camp in La Roche Girls School, Nantes, in the Pays de la Loire region. He sent Dolly a photograph of himself with 16 fellow soldiers in an elegant looking cloister, which was part of the school in which they had been billeted. Presumably the girls had been evicted. Fortunately, there was no need for much marching or shooting there: it was a peaceful German

Peter and Dolly Barth, 1941.

Peter Dolly and Annemarie, 1941.

occupation. It was, quite rightly, highly resented by the French. Perhaps because of his age (41) or because of his profession as an accountant, he was put in charge of the camp stores. His job was to source supplies of food, drink and all the other items needed for day to day living. Back in Hamburg, many things had become very difficult to find in the shops during the war, items that were still available in France, however. So Max frequently, almost daily, sent us parcels of food and other items: sausage, cheese, butter, coffee, tea etc. Our mother would occasionally give the postman something out of these parcels "to

Maximilian Barth in Nantes, France, 1941 (middle of back row, tallest head)

keep him sweet".

In late July 1942, Maximilian was given a short spell of leave from his army posting in Nantes. He went back home to Hamburg. Although there had been sporadic bombing of Hamburg by the RAF from the beginning of the war, in early 1942 these raids were getting bigger. Raids by about 100 bombers became more common and by late July, several hundred were involved in each attack. One night (probably 26/27 July), our mother Dolly, put my sister and me to bed. As usual, she had a small suitcase ready packed, standing by the door. Air-raid alarms had started and she could hear the distant sounds of bombs exploding. Dolly decided it would be wiser not to go to bed. She sat on a chair worrying about whether things would get worse. Suddenly something shot past the window with a loud whoosh and hit a neighbouring house. She said to Max, "We must get down to the cellar, this house might be next." Half asleep, my sister and I were taken down to join the other residents already taking refuge in the cellar. Later Dolly and Max went up to the roof, leaving us below. They saw a nearby house hit by an incendiary bomb and catch fire. My mother said, "Oh how it burnt! So quickly! So bright, with the fire ... all fire!!"

It turned out to be a significant bombing raid by over 400 RAF planes, targetting Hamburg's housing areas, rather than the docks and factories. They killed and wounded hundreds of people and burnt out large areas of housing.

*

My Aunt Gertrude (Trudel) Hamelmann, née Barth, one of my father's two sisters, was married to Adam Hamelmann (the details of which are described in Chapter 7). He became the Chief Steward on the luxury liner Cap Arcona, which was a well paid job. Consequently they could afford a beautiful apartment on Uhlenhorster Weg which is four streets south of Zimmerstraße, where we and other members of the family lived. It was a lovely street, leading down to the eastern bank of the Alster. It joins the appropriately named street, Schöne Aussicht (Beautiful View) running alongside the lake. Trudel and Adam had two boys, Werner and Walter. Also, as noted above, Opa Max Barth had recently moved in with them.

Four months earlier on a night in April 1942 (probably 8/9 April) an operation of 272 RAF bombers attacked Hamburg. They targetted mostly residential areas, dropping both incendiary and explosive bombs. This caused fires and destroyed many houses. On this night, when Opa Max was already in bed, a cluster incendiary bomb came through their roof. It ignited in the attic and burnt through their sitting room ceiling. In those days, ceiling voids were generally insulated with peat or other flammable materials. Peat burns well, so the bomblet emerged through the ceiling. It burnt at a temperature of over 1000ºC and with such a bright light that they could hardly look at it. Opa was roused from his bed. He went to the kitchen, fetched a metal coffee pot and filled it with water. He stood on a chair and threw the water at the bomb. He threw several more pots of water at it. That seemed to have dowsed it so Opa pulled the bomb out of the ceiling and dropped it to the floor. However, it was still very hot so he burnt his hand in the process. Werner and Walter took a broom and literally swept the bomb out of the flat into the hallway and threw a sandbag onto it. That put it out completely. A job well done, Opa went back to bed. However other bombs then came through their hall ceiling. The boys, Werner and Walter, managed to extinguish all of them with sandbags that night. There was a strict and obviously necessary regulation in Hamburg at this time, that every house must have sandbags.

Werner discovered that one of the cluster incendiary bombs had not been triggered. The boys had covered it with a sandbag but, as the mechanism had not been fired, it had remained intact. Werner loved mechanical things and was very clever with his hands. So next day, despite the obvious danger, he took it apart very carefully. This bomb consisted of 12 magnesium alloy incendiary bomblets packed together into an iron core. When the bomb hit its target, a spring was released that shot fuses forwards, igniting and scattering the 12 bomblets. But this one had not fired: the iron core and fuses were still there and the top was intact. He examined the mechanism very carefully to make sure he understood it, then cleaned and polished it. Next day, very bravely I think, he took it to school to show his class mates: it caused a sensation. What the teachers thought, if they knew about it, is not recorded (any acccident could have set the school on fire).

Trudel was a very caring and house-proud mother. She loved her family and saw it her duty to look after them. She wept when she saw all the damage the incendiary bombs had done to her beautiful home. However, if the family had not been there and successfully put the bombs out, the whole apartment could have been burnt out, as happened in many parts of the city that night. She went round cleaning the furniture and carpets, painting and polishing and getting things back to the way they were before. She had the ceilings repaired and the roof made water-tight again. They were lucky they hadn't lost everything, including their lives.

[The UN Convention on Conventional Weapons, concluded in Geneva in 1980, prohibits the use of incendiary weapons against civilians. However, both sides in the Second World War used them without any constraint.]

Chapter Four

Werner in the Wehrmacht

Ich weiß, wieviel das Menschenleben im Kriege wert ist.
Ich habe Kameraden neben mir fallen sehen. Oh, ich weiß.
Laß mich nicht mehr weiterschreiben, ich kann nicht mehr.

WERNER HAMELMANN, FELDPOST 5.I.1943

(I know how little human life is valued in war.
I have seen comrades fall right by me. Oh, I know.
Don't let me write any more, I can't any more.)

Werner did not have much longer at his school. He wrote (3.4.1942) to his father Adam Hamelmann who was on his ship Cap Arcona berthed in the bay of Gdynia in the Baltic Sea. Werner thanks him profusely for the large present he received for getting good marks in his Abitur (final school exams/matriculation). He writes that he hasn't earned it but feels he can now go into the military with a clear conscience. He hasn't received his call-up papers yet but expects them any day because some of his school friends have already been enlisted or been given war-work. He was 18 and didn't have

Edgar Koschel and Werner Hamelmann in Krakau, 1941.

long to wait. Two weeks later (19.4.1942) on a postcard from Rendsburg, on the Kiel canal, north of Hamburg, he announced that "Zwar bin ich jetzt schon Soldat..." "I really am a soldier now (with an old uniform) although I don't feel like one yet". The following month (25.5.1942), from an Ortsunterkunft (military quarters), he writes endlessly about the parcels he has received from home containing cigarettes, cakes, chocolates, German sausage etc. One would think the army didn't feed him at all, although he praises the canteen and his comfortable bed there. He loves getting lots of letters from the family and writes very long letters himself. He must be in Denmark now because he asks them to send him some Danish Krone, if possible, because "without money there is nothing to buy here."

After the Whitsun break, as an exercise, alarms go off in the middle of the night. The recruits are then given half an hour to get themselves completely ready to leave with their battle pack, fire arms, munitions, etc. Their monkey jackets and all their other equipment has to be packed and ready for action. He expects that they will be sent to Hadersleben (Haderslev) in Denmark and hopes they can stay there. The worst aspect is they will march there, a distance of 60 km, with all their pack and munitions. Last time they did a night march of 25 km, "they crept along like rats". They had to drag a machine gun case weighing 60 pounds with them. As a result Werner had 12 blisters on his feet. The blisters have now gone and his feet have hardened up. He got himself some fine new boots and now "runs in them like a young god". He reports he has had a bit of luck: at an inspection, his overalls were so clean that he was excused any further duties that day. Except, he *was* given the job of cleaning and polishing a machine gun so that it gleamed like new and was ready for inspection. That sounds like a contradiction until one thinks that, with his flair for mechanical things, he would enjoy doing the job and would do it exceptionally well.

A few days later Werner writes from Haderslev, Denmark: the move has taken place. No sooner is he there than letters and parcels of chocolate, cigarettes and pralines start arriving from the family. He thanks them for these goodies and for always thinking of him and writing. He also gets a letter from a school friend, Carli, who seems to have been lucky in getting war-work in an office which suits him very well. On Sunday, Werner and his fellow recruits were given leave to wander around the town. As he had no Danish Krone he sold a couple of packets of cigarettes to a "not quite sober" chap who immediately invited them to have a glass of beer with him. Although Werner confesses "he had a very dry throat", he decides to go back to camp to write letters instead. He doesn't feel at all well after the terrible march from their last camp to Haderslev and thinks he should book into the sick-bay the following day. However the countryside and town are better than their last stop, although they are now in a converted school which is obviously more primitive than their previous barracks. The march was 70 km long, taken in two stages; it was the worst he had ever experienced in his life. His feet are kaput but he hopes to get used to these marches. Then he writes "Nie wieder Krieg!!!" * ("Never again War!!!"). "But a private must keep such thoughts to himself and not say a word. In a hundred years there will be no more wars."

The following day, 1 June 1942, Werner went to see the doctor. He was diagnosed with angina and ordered a sweating cure. He was sent straight to bed so he had time enough to write a long letter to his mother and Opa Max. It is mostly about money, buying shoes and selling cigarettes to the Danes. He needs some razor blades. "They are expensive in Denmark but I need them soon because my beard has grown so long, it gets tangled between my legs". At the beginning of July he is still in Denmark but wonders how long for. It turns out to be not very long: they were training to harden themselves up a bit before the real fighting starts. Werner, it seems, needed the toughening up. Two weeks later he springs a big surprise on his family at home in Hamburg. After three months of training in Denmark as a raw recruit, he has already been sent to Russia. In a letter from "Bleskau" (presumably Pleskau = Pleskov = Pskov) he writes:

(15.7.1942): We have crossed the Russian border. The landscape here is bleak and disconsolate and the Lithuanian and Latvian landscapes are dull, boggy and wooded, yet one cannot see that war has crossed these lands. The people here are terribly stubborn. Tomorrow we will reach our objective, perhaps Leningrad. I hope the RAF will not strike at targets in the Baltic again, especially as my mother (Trudel) and brother (Walter) are visiting our father on the Cap Arcona.

The ship is berthed in the Bay of Gotenhafen (Gdynia) in the Baltic Sea. There have also been big air attacks on Hamburg. Werner writes to his mother:

(3. 8.1942): I am so pleased to get news from home

that the family is safe because, where we are now, we are completely cut off from broadcast news. We could listen to a wireless in Denmark but not here. We eat pretty well. On Sunday, with our meal, we had beer, Schnaps, real coffee, and sweets. In the evening we were served milk soup. It was a very enjoyable evening before we crawled into our tents. I have booked myself onto a radio-communication operator's course. Now and again we see planes. Yesterday afternoon a Russian bomber with two fighter planes suddenly appeared above us. There was a burst of gunfire from our camp, the bomber caught fire, rumbled on and crashed nearby. Parachutes appeared in the sky so we had go out to hunt for the men. One of them was caught but the others escaped. I thought, there are interesting things happening here. It's a pity the weather is so changeable.

The Siege of Leningrad

Whether he found it "interesting" or not, Werner had in fact been sent as part of the German forces to the Siege of Leningrad which had started almost a year before his arrival, in September 1941. This was when the Wehrmacht sealed the city off from the south while the Finnish army invaded from the north. The Finns had some justification for their action: they recaptured territory seized by the Russians in the Winter War of 1939. This was the only reason they had taken part and, having achieved it, they ceased any further military action. They refused German requests to attack Leningrad from the north. But they did effectively continue to act as a siege barrier to Russian movement to the north. The attack by the Germans from the south was a completely unjustified. It was a perfideous one-sided break of the 1939 Non-Aggression Pact between Hitler and Stalin (which Hitler had no intention of honouring). Leningrad was sealed in. It became the longest and most murderous siege known in history. Many historians regard it as an act of genocide. Over one million victims of the siege lie buried in the Leningrad cemetery, most of whom died of starvation. The death toll, including soldiers, is thought to be about one and a half million. Hitler's intentions were to destroy the city and its inhabitants utterly. He ordered that requests for surrender were to be ignored. It is said that Hitler was so sure of success that he had invitations printed for the victory celebrations, to be held in Leningrad's grand Hotel Astoria.

A week after Werner's last letter, on the 9 August 1942, Shostakovich's Symphony No 7 "Leningrad" was performed in the city by a half-starved orchestra, under the very difficult circumstances of the siege. Shostakovich started writing it while acting as a fire warden for the Leningrad Conservatory. He had been rejected by the army because of his poor eyesight. (What a blessing that was for the musical legacy he left the world.) He was evacuated with his family from Leningrad in October 1941, not long after the start of the siege. He completed the symphony in Samara (southern Russia). The score was microfilmed and sent to New York where Toscanini gave a famous performance which was broadcast around the world. It became, and remains, a powerful tribute to the bravery and resistance of the Russians under siege in Leningrad.

[My wife Jane and I went to Leningrad in April 1987 on a school trip of teachers and pupils, organized by Tarporley High School, where Jane taught English and Drama. We were welcomed there by Russian teachers and pupils. They showed us around the magnificent Winter Palace Square, churches and other beautiful features of the city. One sunny afternoon, but with snow still on the ground and ice floating down the Neva, we were taken to the Piskaryovkoye Cemetary. We saw where almost a million dead victims of the siege had been buried in long trench graves. Back in the city, at the House of Friendship (just off Nevsky Prospekt near the Dom Knigi) we were shown a film with original footage of the siege. The music of Shostakovich's 7th Symphony accompanied these harrowing images: it was impossible not to shed tears.]

*

Two days after the premier of this symphony in Leningrad, Werner wrote to his family:

(11. 8. 1942): On Sunday, after a glittering manoeuvre from our old camp, we marched to the battle front. One goes there with mixed feelings, like going on holiday. So we marched on and were suddenly under a fierce attack. As you know, I am now the regiment's radio operator together with a colleague from Denmark. We moved on next morning and discovered a fine bunker where we could hold out from the attack. You have to have luck in the army. There were many other soldiers in there already. It was safe and quiet. Now and again we could hear artillery or mortar bombs but otherwise everything is alright here, you need not worry about me.

A few days later he wrote:

(16. 8. 1942): Just imagine, I have been a Front soldier for a whole week now and I am feeling better day by day, even though the word Front is generally connected with terrible fatigue. However, if we had been ordered to join in the battle at Volkhov, then we would have had a different notion of the word Front. Very few of our soldiers came back from there alive. We have the impression that not much will happen here but in the south, the troops still have an immense advance to make. When we get to the Volga, a strong "wall" will be built. Then the Russians will

have to give up because we will have cut them off from their essential life-supports. We only hope the winter won't be as harsh as it apparently was last year. I think an attack on Moscow or Leningrad is unlikely. We are preparing everything necessary for the winter and hope our position will hold." He describes life at the front as being not so bad, "although after a year here one would become stubborn and stupid. We have alcohol, cigarettes and cinema shows in the regimental barracks. The feeling of camaraderie is good and yesterday we received a bottle of Sekt (sparkling wine) each and chocolate pudding on Sunday. Pity we have no wireless to listen to. If you could send me a couple of newspapers and a magazine I would be very pleased. I also need a pair of shoe insoles and sugar to make jam from all the fruit (berries) around here. (Werner often reveals his love of sweet things.)

A couple of days later he writes that the Russians had started shelling the village where their bunker is. The house next to them went up in flames. At first they thought they were still safe but then, full of sound and fury, heavy munition hit the bunker which cracked and groaned. They all grabbed their kit and got out fast. It was just in time, because then:

(18. 8.1942): 400 grenades flew through the air, with an earsplitting noise. I was thrown the length of the building on my stomach. Around midnight half the village was in flames. This made it a clear target for further attack from the Russians as we could be seen in the dark. We escaped from the village with one soldier wounded but no one killed. The bunker was then hit by 18 hand-grenades which sent it into the air and burnt it out completely. Next morning we went back to reconstruct an old bunker. There was nothing much left of the village except a few chimney stacks.

This was followed by a merciful lull in the fighting. Werner discusses the war with his father Adam Hamelmann, on the Cap Arcona. Werner writes:

(20. 8. 1942): I believe a strong "wall" will be built from the Volga down to the south which the Russians won't be able to penetrate. Here in the north there is nothing more to do: the territory behind Leningrad is worthless to us. We will hope for the best, that the war will end soon. Our opponents have little to gain and I believe that, after the terrible disaster of the English landing at Dieppe, they will also think again about the continuation of the war. Because England is losing such a great tonnage of shipping in the Atlantic, I wonder if they will stop fighting. An invasion by them now seems unlikely. We hope for victory soon.

The "Dieppe Raid" took place on 19 August 1942 (so Werner must have received this information very soon after it happened, presumably from a Wehrmacht broadcast). The raid was a complete disaster. An invasion force of over 6,000 troops, mostly Canadian, made a beach landing to capture the port of Dieppe. The Germans were well prepared and in six hours, most of the invading forces had been killed or captured. A retreat was called. The RAF lost over 100 planes to 48 by the Luftwaffe. The only straw of comfort to the Allies was that this served as a lesson for the subsequent successful Normandy Landings in June 1944.

Werner describes his life in the army in Russia:

(21. 8. 1942): The regimental camp has a cinema, where we saw *Bel Ami*. We were also treated to a performance of music by the Regimental Band followed by a supper of soup and rolls. I never imagined that things like this would exist at the Front. They do everything imaginable for the

soldiers. The barracks are very comfortable. But what I miss is letters from you. My comrades talk a lot about what they will do when the war is over and how they will live their lives. We hope that time is not far away. What I miss most is mental occupation: during my whole time in the army, I have not read a single book. Perhaps that time will come soon. The plague of vermin and midges has become so great a curse that you spend night and day scratching. In the evening you don't get a minute's peace from them and at night you have to pull the sheets over your head otherwise you wake up in the morning with a fat face.

In another letter to his family he writes:

(20. 9. 1942): You seem to be worried that I have taken to drink. I can assure you that, during my entire time in the army, I have never been tipsy or drunk and that when we are given alcohol, it is such foul-tasting hooch, it gives me the shakes. Recently 12 of us got together and acquired a very fine bottle of apricot brandy. Of course, we only drank one small glassful each. I would have been keen to drink more of it and so would you, I think. We are very busy now reorganizing everything for the winter which is on its way. We are building a sauna but we don't know if we will be staying here. We will wait and drink tea. The Russians have become very active again, particularly in the air. They fly over at night in their "Iron Gustav" which is an armour-plated bomber. They drop bombs on us and then machine gun our positions. However, I find that bomb attacks on our homes in Hamburg are far, far more terrifying than this. I feel reassured when Hamburg is not mentioned in the Wehrmacht reports.

Towards the end of September 1942 the Battle of Stalingrad

started with German and other Axis forces attacking the Soviet Union for control of this southern city. Werner makes no mention of this. It turned into a ghastly blood-bath on both sides. Many letters follow, dealing with Werner's love of sweet foods, books and family matters, while reassuring them that all is well with him in Russia. He writes to his family:

(22. 10. 1942): I have been sent on a radio-operators' course for a week, well away from the war. We are not directly close to Leningrad now but in a "pocket" which obviously you must know nothing about. Many rumours are circulating around the camp that:- 1) we will stay in this quiet spot away from the front, 2) Leningrad will now be captured, 3) we will be sent to the south of France, or 4) sent to Norway. But you can't believe any of this humbug, no one actually knows. We got half a bar of chocolate each today, which is always a good omen.

Werner was on watch and due to be relieved in the middle of the night. He wrote another letter to Trudel, his mother:

(21.11.1942): It was dreadful! We had to take down some cables at night, during snow storms and heavy shooting. It was a crazy muddle. Next morning we got going, marching and marching. In the evening we reached our quarters where we were going to do some training before we moved forward. On 19 November we marched away from the Front. The shooting grew ever quieter. We reached the village we would stay in that evening. I was surprised to see for the first time an immense pile of parcels. The whole squadron made themselves comfortable. Then came my birthday on 20 November. Well, what can I say? We were busy all day but it was still my birthday. I thought about my home and last year, how it was always so good there and how it has turned out this time. But that doesn't matter, I was always so lucky that you, at home, have always thought about me with love. Now we have left our nice camp and no one knows what is going to happen to us so soon before Chistmas. One thing is certain: we are leaving the northern war-sector (Leningrad) and there is a lot of talk about the middle war-sector: Norway, France, Germany or God knows where? All our furlough for Christmas has vanished. Well, we wanted to be surprised! We have been thoroughly deloused and that really means something. Wait!! We will learn about it soon enough. Now we are 20 men in a small hut but there is no shooting outside, although it is cold. So, my surprise present to you arrived on your birthday? That made me so happy, I wanted so much to pay you back a little. You will hear from me again very soon.

He sounds thoroughly upset about about missing a break at Christmas. In his next letter (26.11.1942) Werner describes their full winter clothing: a fur coat, wadded under-trousers and a thick lined muff. "When it's cold, stormy and snowing, we won't freeze. We are working very hard at the moment but that doesn't surprise us old privates. Hopefully we will, at least, have the opportunity to celebrate Christmas."

His last letter of the year (24.12.1942) is a long one, full of nostagia about the wonderful Christmases they had at home. How they decorated the Christmas tree and had presents under it, made marzipan and baked cakes. Their walls were decorated with photographs attached to serviettes. Finally came the moment when he and his brother Walter, were allowed into the room to see all the wonderful presents and sweeties. In their hut, in the snow in Russia, they did their best to recreate the atmosphere of Christmas. They cleared a space in the middle. Around the walls they put up Christmas tree branches and photos they had received from home. They had cigarettes, chocolate, a bottle of Sekt, biscuits, sweets and gingerbread. The wireless played soft music. They all reminisced about how they celebrated Christmas at home and how much they wanted to be there. "This is the first and hopefully also the last Christmas on the battle-field. By the middle of next year I will certainly be allowed leave. By the way, this evening I was surprised to be told that I would be promoted to lance-corporal."

Werner's first long letter to his mother in the New Year was confessional but covering a brutal time at the Front:

(5.1.1943): In my letters I have given you the impression that we were involved in some sort of child's play. I believe I have, from the beginning, misled you about what was happening here in the east. I have been on duty in Russia from the start, forward at the Front. I had the luck to be in a very safe position where the Russians were encircled and completely powerless. Since 25 November there has been an enormous defensive slaughter (Abwehrschlacht) going on and we, as a strong fighting force, were thrown in. (The double-think involved in the phrase "defensive slaughter" is very chilling: the Germans are not defending anything, they *attacked* Leningrad!) It has not been easy for four weeks, but pure gold in the last few days. We, as radio operators with a small unit, were pulled out and thrown into a position where the Russians had broken through. At night we made a counterthrust to reestablish the connection at least. That was my first attack, which anyone who came out of it alive, will never forget. We lay for 8 days in a snow hollow until there was nothing left of the battalion and then we were pulled out. We were rescued last night and now we are lying here in the Tross (baggage train) with a couple of men who are making us as comfortable as they can. (A Tross seems to be more a sort of Trost, a comfort station, a mobile hotel, kitchen, hospital and recuperation refuge, rather than just a train carrying baggage.)

In the snow hollow we had no roof over our heads and the temperature was a few degrees below zero. We couldn't dig ourselves in because the ground was frozen hard. Only Schnaps could hold us up, otherwise we would have felt awful for those days, but, with moral hindsight, we got over it. I can't say any more or else I will be thrown in the clink again. I escaped from a direct hit in my snow hollow with my skin intact, how, I don't know myself. It's a hard lesson for later in life: one sees it with different eyes.

It was around this time that Werner, under attack, found shelter from the onslaught in a fox hole. He was amazed to find a Russian soldier already in there! The bombardment was so heavy that neither of them could do anything but keep their heads well down until it eased off. Neither tried to attack the other, instead they chatted until it seemed safe to come out again and go their own ways. This was an anecdote he told us after the war. It was not the sort of thing he could write in his letters home because of army censorship. He had obviously self-censored his letters, as above, where he admits he "will be thrown in the clink again" for revealing too much of what is going on in Russia. He also tries not to worry his mother too much as she was naturally fearful about losing her beloved son. It is clear from his response to her letters that she always feared the worst so, usually, he made light of the danger he was in. But his experience of being trapped in the snow hollow for eight days was life-changing. He writes to his mother:

(5. 1. 1943): I know how little human life is valued in war. I have seen my comrades fall next to me. Oh I know, I must stop, I cannot write any more. I'll write again soon.

Werner was 19 years old.

Chapter Five

Werner in Russia 1943

Wir haben einen Angriff gemacht, und Du kannst Dir
denken, daß er, da er mit unendlichen Schwierigkeiten
verbunden war, seelisch und auch köperlich Spuren
hinterlassen hat. Man kann das schlecht schildern, wie einem
dabei zumute ist, wenn man den sicheren Tod schon im
Auge gesehen hat, Ihr werdet es schlecht begreifen können.
WERNER HAMELMANN: FELDPOST 18.4.1943

(We made an attack and, you know what, it left us
bound with unending difficulties, both mental and
physical. It is difficult to describe, as one is expected
to, when one has looked certain death in the eye, it is
difficult to understand.)

Werner was given a couple of days recuperation on the
baggage train (Tross). He is happy that the Russians are
quiet at the moment (17.1.1943). He is now fully occupied in
the construction of a bunker in their new position. The work
has the advantage that it keeps them warm. He thanks his

mother for all the lovely presents he received over Christmas, cakes, cigarettes, gloves, newspapers and magazines. He is still a basic radio-operator, no promotion yet, but he hopes to get onto another course and move up the ranks. Another couple of letters in January follow the same themes of "Food and Fate". He receives parcels with salmon, pralines, sausage and a shawl that acts as a great "louse-catcher". "Nobody knows what Fate has in store for us so don't get grey hairs worrying about it." Werner hopes that his mother will go to the Pfalz away from Hamburg, it will be safer there. He is very grateful for all the parcels, "But please only send those things that you can do without." They have a new warm bunker with a wireless. The Russians seem to have gone quiet and moved their resistance further south. He expects a new (German) offensive in the spring and then surely the war must finish! "Heads up, and never despair."

Building bunkers was a full-time army occupation at this time; anyway, it keeps them warm and busy when the shooting stops. Werner still seems to have piles of parcels coming in frequently (marzipan, almonds and cake). One contained his glasses which he had broken and sent back to Germany: they were now mended. Although it is only February, spring is in the air. In the summer the ground they are on will become a large marsh and they will have to move on. Werner reassures his mother that all is quiet at the moment. There is a great deal of interest among the troops about the future, about a victorious end to the war. The inculcation of Nazi fervour ("holy duty") into the troops is horrifyingly obvious in his next letter:

(1. 2. 1943): You know about it as much as I do but one thing I can say is: it will happen in this year. We will find ourselves in total war. For every German it is self-evident and a holy duty that, in our Stalingrad battle, we will go to any extreme for victory. And it is for us a relief when we know that all the young fellows who have been called

up, and have now left their pleasures behind, can also see a bit more of the world. How many of them are there? And how many young, childless women haven't known for a long time what they should do all day? I won't name names but you know as well as I do, there are too many of them, and these are the ones who are complaining the most. Why should only soldiers fight here and sacrifice themselves for the same person who sits at home all day on their lazy arse.

It is not so bad for us; we have to accept our heavy losses. However, I have the firm conviction that, in the coming summer, it will be favourable for us. The Russians will be destroyed, at any rate such that they can no longer create difficulties for us. This presumes, of course, that everyone does their utmost. And when you or grandpa are asked to help with any sort of work, you must do it: the sacrifice our soldiers have made for their homeland, obliges everyone to help. It affects us all at this crucial time and everyone must be clear about it.

Werner and a colleague were given five evenings in the Tross. They took some of the food Werner had received in his parcels and cooked it there. In his latest letter he writes:

(12. 2. 1943): The greatest happiness we got was from being deloused! These little creatures were literally on my heart, i.e. living in my shirt. It was an amazing feeling to be fully louse-free. Thank God, I say! After a somewhat less than comfortable trip in a lorry through the snow-covered roads, we arrived after 12 hours in Staraya Russa (a town about 200 km south of Leningrad, near Lake Ilmen) and then went by train to our new garrison. It's quite a large town and we have warm accommodation. Unfortunately it hasn't got a cinema or soldiers' home.

Another disadvantage is that the food is not as good as at our last camp. But we'll get used to it, especially as we are now far from the shooting.

He has gone there for another radio-operator's course. Not much is going on in their new garrison and Werner is missing the post from home (15. 2.1943). However, he is "blessed with heavenly peace. There are no howling grenades, the organ is not being played, no bombs are whistling, it is so strange." He hopes that summer will come soon. "We won't get a furlough this summer, but that doesn't matter because the war must end soon and then we can catch up." His optimism seems irrepressible but one should not forget that his letters home were intended to keep his mother (Trudel) from worrying too much about him. He writes to her (30. 3.1943), "By the way, have you heard on the Wehrmacht news report that, on the whole of the eastern Front, there is only local fighting going on? That's a massive thing, we couldn't wish for anything better."

April brought better weather. Werner asked his mother to keep his letters, as they will always be a wonderful memory of these days. Little did he know that nearly 80 years later I would be translating them for a book about his and other family members' lives during the war years. Unfortunately, but perhaps not surprisingly, he was forced to destroy some of his letters for security or propaganda reasons. This should be taken into account when everything *seems* to be going so well for them in Russia. He writes to his mother:

(2. 4. 1943): Your latest letter made me very happy as you sound a bit more optimistic now. You always thought that I was at the Front in the worst fighting but I am here in peace and quiet now. It is always different from what you think. They have no room for us at the Front, it is completely full. We have lovely weather at the moment,

quite warm. Our airmen drive around here in their jeeps. It is such a delight to see the Stukas flying over us in unbroken swarms, away to unload their bombs while not letting the Russians see them coming. Recently, four Russian bombers flew towards us but, before they had reached our camp, our fighters were behind them firing their guns. In less then two minutes all four bombers had been hit. They crashed in flames without having dropped any bombs. It's fun to watch aerial battles.

The good weather seems to have raised their spirits. Werner loved Trudel's previous letter, he read it umpteen times. He replies:

(6. 4. 1943): I was really astonished by your last letter. It had a different voice to previous ones which were usually so sad, while this one has a really happy voice. Here the frost has gone already and we can go outside in shirt-sleeves now. I want to be at home with you all and listen to your "mouth-watering plans" for a holiday. Look after your health. Go for lots of walks and lie on the balcony in the sun. Above all, stop all that unnecessary hard work of scouring and polishing your floorboards this year, or else, when I come home on leave, I will trample all over them with my soldier's boots on. By the way, you *can* eat horse meat, it doesn't taste bad. But not wild horse meat, that's far too tough. Recruits into the armed forces are getting ever younger, 15 year olds will be on the Front soon! No, it won't really get that bad. It is good that the ones who were shirking will now get to see a little of the war. Schoolboys now support the Flak (Flugzeugabwehrkanone = anti-aircraft guns) in the towns, which releases very many soldiers for the eastern Front. Walter, you will definitely have to help with the harvest this summer.

Parcels of wonderful cakes continue to arrive. Werner apologises for not writing for a week. He has been through another near-death trauma that he needs to deal with:

(18. 4. 1943): You can't lie to your inner-self: you will never get things straight if you do not dare to express what you wish to say. I have never censored myself and have always written the truth, as expected of me. Indeed I have always endeavoured to keep a friendly smile, if I can say that, and above all, never lose my sense of humour. You will now be saying to yourselves, what *is* he on about? It is this: we were at the Front recently and made an attack, and you know what, it left us bound with unending difficulties, both mental and physical. It is difficult to describe as one is expected to, when one has looked certain death in the eyes. It is difficult to understand. I won't write any details, I really can't.

Anyway, all went well with our radio so we will now be left in peace for a long time. You will understand that I could not write immediately, we had to recover, which we will do in the fullness of time. A small surprise is that I have to write a short report about what happened in the attack and this will be broadcast on the wireless. It was a significant event with new weapons with unheard of capabilities. Perhaps you will hear the broadcast: that would be nice. I must stop here, otherwise I will think about it too much.

When they got back to base-camp, they were greeted with food, drink, cigarettes and light music on the wireless. On Sunday they are going to be treated to asparagus, braised beef and potatoes with wonderful gravy and finishing with a vanilla dessert. They are back near Leningrad but life there doesn't seem to be too bad at the moment. What a contrast from the lives of the Russians they are starving to death by siege in the city.

Easter in Russia is a time for nostalgia about the Easter festivals at home. Werner recalls the Easter egg hunt in the morning, a wonderful lunch and then the whole family (bar one) out for a lovely Easter walk. That means, of course, that his mother, Trudel, is left doing all the clearing away and washing up at home and then preparing the supper. It fits with the old German adage that the duty of women is "Kinder, Kirche und Küche" (children, church and kitchen). In their base-camp in Russia the German troops are lucky being in a quiet spot, giving them, as the carol has it: heavenly peace, and a chance to recover from their hangovers. There is a delay before Werner's next letter arrives. He apologises to his mother and thanks her for her letter and parcel which he hasn't yet opened.

(3. 6. 1943): This is because something happened which I will tell you about. We were finishing building the block houses and I had a small unfortunate accident. While carrying a beam, a branch caught me in the eye and got stuck there. I went around for a day with a swimming, leaking eye until it got worse and of course, it hurt a lot. I went to our medical orderly but he couldn't do anything, so he sent me to the eye doctor in the field hospital. The eye is not too bad now. I have a small slit in the cornea now and I am spending a couple of lovely days here. I was knocked off my feet to see this spacious establishment so close to the Front. The medical care is outstanding. I didn't bring anything with me except a couple of letters, so yesterday evening I went to the cinema and, I must say, if life goes on like this, I could happily spend a couple of months here. However in 2 – 4 days my stay here will be over. Even so, it has been a wonderful opportunity to eat my fill and sleep well. What more could anyone want?

In the next letter to his mother, Werner writes that he is still in the military hospital and can't just sleep all day, so he has been putting his things in order. More parcels arrive including a bottle of egg liqueur which he is very pleased with. Trudel obviously made it herself because he tells her off for using her few precious eggs just for him. However, he will be able to sip a little of this costly liquid if he can get some time again in the Tross.

Werner stayed in Russia until the end of June 1943, which meant he had spent a whole year there. In that time approximately 250,000 German troops had been killed in the Siege of Leningrad. He was probably not aware of that. The chance of his still being alive after this time was not great, a fact that he would not have shared with his mother if he knew it. Throughout his time there, he was always careful not to worry her any more than possible: Trudel was a natural pessimist (or possibly a realist).

After his spell of duty in Russia, Werner was sent on furlough to peaceful Denmark for a couple of weeks. He and some colleagues had a great time there, especially at his favourite pastime it seems: eating. On the 8th of July they got their marching orders and on the 9th, went for a break in Hamburg. Werner wrote to his family:

(12.7.1943): We had calculated that we were due 14 days leave, but to our annoyance we were informed that we must go back the next day. I had it all planned that I would get home in the afternoon. However, I had to stay on duty. I immediately phoned home and my mother (Trudel) was flabbergasted. The next day my mother, Walter and Opa came to see me and we had a good time together. When it was time to go, all three of them came with us to the station. The moment of departure was emotionally very difficult but I suppose that was inevitable. Let's hope it works out soon. The lovely two weeks are gone but we'll think about them. You can't get strawberry tart in Russia. Today, after two day's travel we are now in Graudenz (Grudziadz in Poland) and had to wait here for a day. This town is very depressing, Polish and swarming with police. We went to a terrible cinema and now we are eating even more terrible food. This evening we move on and in six days time we'll be back at base-camp.

They got back to Russia only to be given, almost immediately, the leave that they had, in fact, been entitled to. What a waste of travelling time: this doesn't sound much like German efficiency! So Werner had to travel all the way back to Hamburg again to spend the furlough with his family. He got away from the battle front but it did not turn out to be the peaceful break he was expecting.

Chapter Six

The Bombing of Hamburg 1943

"They sowed the wind and now they
are going to reap the whirlwind."

<small>Air Chief Marshal Sir Arthur Travis (Bomber) Harris, 1942.</small>

In late July 1943, my cousin Werner Hamelmann was enjoying a few days leave with his family in Hamburg. His parents, Adam and Trudel, decided to throw a party on his last day there, on Saturday the 24th of July 1943 (an inauspicious day as you will see). Werner's brother Walter, recently recruited into the army at the age of 16, was given leave to come. We, the Barth family, were invited: my mother Dolly, sister Annemarie and me.

Peter, Dolly and Annemarie Barth, Hamburg, June 1943.

Sadly, our father Maximilian could not get furloughed from his army post at the Lüneburg Camp. Our grandfather Opa Max came along. The Koschel family: Else (Trudel's sister), her husband Richard and their daughter Rosi were also invited. Adam and Trudel booked a table at the beautiful cafe in Planten un Blomen, the large Pleasure Gardens near the Alster, where we could all enjoy a traditional German Kaffee und Kuchen (coffee and cakes) party in the sunny weather. There was a fine bandstand near by which, before the war, was used for coffee-dances, but Hitler had forbidden such pleasures. He said, "Why should people at home enjoy themselves dancing when men at the front were fighting for their fatherland?"

In Planten un Blomen, we were close to the Binnen Alster, the smaller part of the Alster Lake, adjoining the city centre. It had been camouflaged with floating fake buildings, streets and canals. This was constructed to confuse enemy aircraft as to where the city centre actually was.

We had a very happy reunion in the Gardens before the war split us up again. It was a great occasion for Werner to do what he loved most: to talk with his family, drink coffee and eat the delicious cakes provided. He was particularly fond of cakes and sweet things, as mentioned already, although he always managed, amazingly, to retain his slim healthy figure. As the weather was so warm and sunny, there were many people in the café and wandering happily in the parks around the Alster. Werner, who was then 19, looked around him at the other people in the cafe. A flash of anger came over him when he noticed young men not in uniform who were a similar age to him. He presumed they were still civilians, enjoying the sunshine and freedom, while *he* had to go back to the war front in Russia the following day. However, being with his family made him happy and the moment passed. Werner had a lot to say about his time in Russia. He was an excellent story teller, always interesting and entertaining, with an infectious optimism. It was a very enjoyable gathering of nearly all the family: a good chance to talk about what we had all been doing and the state of the country in wartime. Although we did not know it then, it was to be our last chance for such an occasion in Hamburg for a long time. As the evening drew on, it was time for us to go home. We all kissed and hugged and said our farewells, hoping to meet again soon.

At about 9 pm that night, 24 July 1943, the sirens in Hamburg sounded. Our mother took my sister and me down into the cellar of our apartment block in Zimmerstraße. We were used to this now, we had done it many times before. On previously nights, a few planes dropped some incendiary and explosive bombs on Hamburg and then flew on. We saw search lights across the sky and flak fired from the many defence stations. But this night was going to be very different: it was the first attack of Operation Gomorrah. Bombers took off from several airfields on the east coast of England and flew across the North Sea, heading apparently for Denmark to mislead the German defence fighter planes. About 100 km from the coast of north Germany, 791 RAF bombers arrived at carefully timed intervals. They turned south-east forming a vast phalanx of planes over 300 km long, heading towards Hamburg. Pathfinder aircraft went ahead and dropped colour-coded marker flares on the route and on target zones of the city.

On this night the bombers, approaching from the north-west, attacked mainly the western half of Hamburg. The city was severely bombed, including the districts of Hoheluft, Eimsbuttel, Altona, St Pauli and Neustadt. In the centre of the old city, in the narrow streets, an ancient six-story house that Brahms was born in, and lived in for many years, was bombed and destroyed by fire. There was significant bomb damage to the docks area which was important for both the navy and merchant shipping. In the extensive harbour area, U-boat and ship construction docks, as well as the armaments factories and warehouses in the industrial districts, were badly damaged. Some of the bombs fell short onto the countryside on the approach route by a process called creep-back. This happens because each wave of bombers sees the explosions and flames of the previous bombing wave and then drops their bombs a bit sooner so as not to bomb the same area. It was the first of three major and one minor night air raids on Hamburg by the RAF. We lived on the eastern side of the Alster so, in this operation, only one or two bombs fell in our district of Uhlenhorst. About 1,500 people were killed in this, the first Gomorrah air raid.

That morning after that night-time attack, on Sunday, 25 July, Werner had to be at the Hamburg Hauptbahnhof (main train station) for his journey back to Russia. His father Adam went with him, carrying his suitcase. Werner carried his heavy military radio equipment. They were both under orders to be armed but neither of them had been issued with a gun. As they got nearer to the centre of Hamburg, where the bombing had ocurred, a terrible sight met their eyes: the station and many other buildings around it were still on fire from the night before. Bomb destruction debris was scattered everywhere. Burnt and blackened corpses were lying in the streets. Dead bodies were stuck to the roads by melted tar. It was an unspeakably horrifying scene of death and destruction. Some time after this, Werner wrote, with his usual irony, he knew that his Führer needed his self-sacrifice in Russia. Later, he discovered that Wehrmacht regulations would have permitted him to take some leave at that time, under rules that applied when his home town had been bombed. However, incredible as it would have seemed to him then, staying in Hamburg would have been in fact *more* dangerous than going to the eastern Front in Russia. Of course Werner did not know this and felt helpless at having to leave his family. He had his orders. There was only one train waiting in the station: destination Berlin. He climbed on board. Pressing his thumbs for luck and with a "stone on his heart" he said goodbye to his father.

Werner missed the following attack on Hamburg later that same day. In the afternoon the bombing started again, but this time, by the American USAAF. They decided to carry out bombing missions only in daylight hours because the better visibility enabled them to avoid the housing areas of the city: they were morally opposed to killing civilians unnecessarily. The daylight also enabled them to see the military installations in the docks and factories and bomb them more accurately. Through technical advances, their bombing precision was now much better than that of the RAF which had barely improved since WW1. The Boeing B-17 "Flying Fortresses" flew in tight formations at a record-beating height of about 10 km and were bristling with guns so that, during the flight to their target, they were almost impregnable. The burning ruins of Hamburg were easily visible as they came lower on their approach. Although the smoke obscured some of the docks areas they were seeking, they made successful major hits on dockyards and armaments factories. The Luftwaffe fighters attacked them in great numbers and proved that the Fortresses were no longer impregnable under these conditions. Fifteen USAAF planes were shot down and many more damaged in that raid.

Despite the significant loss of aircraft and airmen, the USAAF mission was repeated the following day, 26 July, because the weather was so clear. However, there was an extraordinarily high drop-out rate of the American airmen. They were fatigued, had had very little sleep and now knew what awaited them. So in the second USAAF mission, fewer squadrons of bombers set off to repeat their attack on Hamburg. By this time the docks had been deliberately hidden by smoke-screens which the Germans set up all around the area. Bomb aiming became less effective. After dropping their bombs, the Americans looped round for the long journey back to England. Apart from the warning sirens going off, most of us residents in Hamburg were little aware of these out of town raids on the docks and factories.

There was no let-up in the bombing raids, day or night. It was thought that the constant bombing and deprivation of sleep would break the population's morale. On the evening of 27 July 1943, the RAF started their second Gomorrah night attack on Hamburg. Air-raid sirens sounded again. By this time our mother had been told to use a better bomb shelter than the cellar under our house. After the severity of the first Gomorrah attack, the authorities organized the availability of more secure shelters. There weren't any concrete bunkers near us but we were allocated spaces in the crypt of the local church, the Heilandskirche in Winterhuder Weg. Our mother took us briskly the short walk from our home to the church. The crypt had obviously not been built to be bomb-proof, but it was deeper, larger and presumably safer than the small cellar under our apartment block. There were already many people sheltering in there when we arrived. We sat down and made ourselves comfortable.

The weather was unusually warm and clear, giving good visibility to the RAF bombers. As with the first Gomorrah attack, the RAF used a method of confusing German radar. It was code-named "Window" but generally called chaff by the airmen. The Germans had independently devised the same system, called Düppel from the name of the suburb in Berlin where it was first tested. Neither side knew that the other side had developed it. For a long time both sides were reluctant to use it because each thought that the other side would discover its function once it had been used. They would then produce their own chaff and bomb cities more readily. Gomorrah was the first operation in which the RAF had been given permission by the War Office to use it. "Window" consisted of thousands of inch-wide black paper strips covered with aluminium foil on one side. These were cut to a length which was half the wavelength of the radar transmissions used by the Germans in the cities. The strips resonate at the transmission frequency, giving a mass of reflections. Starting near the coast of Germany, Pathfinder aircraft dropped thousands of these strips in bundles every minute as they flew towards Hamburg. The chaff fluttered slowly down to the ground in a cloud, creating a radar fog. Each bomber also posted bundles of this metalic chaff through the flare chute at regular intervals as it flew towards the city. This had the effect of blanking out all the many radar stations protecting Hamburg. Radar-controlled search lights no longer functioned. Radar-predicted anti-aircraft flak guns were disabled and the defence night fighter planes were blinded. This meant that the RAF bombers could attack Hamburg, almost with impunity as they had done on the first attack.

Fires were still burning in many parts of the city from the first mission three nights before. The RAF flew three huge bombing missions at night. On this night, Tuesday, 27th July, as we were sitting in the shelter, the second phase of Operation Gomorrah had just begun. We sat cuddled together, our mother Dolly, my sister Annemarie and me. It was dark, hot, stuffy and crowded in the crypt. A hand-operated pump was being used to bring air into the crypt. People took turns to operate it, but whenever the pumping stopped for a while, the air got hot and sticky again. Air-raid sirens were still sounding outside. Then we heard some distant bomb blasts. All the sirens in Hamburg had been turned on: the whole city seemed to be wailing. Our mother put her arms around us and held us close. I clutched my teddy bear tightly. We didn't know what was happening. The bombing seemed to get louder. We could hear the drone of the planes flying near but not over us. The air was full of sound and fury as bomb explosions continued outside for what seemed to us like hours. In fact, the bomb attack lasted for just over an hour. All we could do was wait and hope for the best. Our mother hugged us both. Everyone in the shelter was silent and frightened.

Squadrons of planes, a total of 787 RAF bombers, flew over Hamburg to continue the destruction they had started during the first Gomorrah attack. This time the planes had looped around the north of Hamburg and came in from the north-east. They attacked the districts of Eilbek, Hohenfelde, Borgfelde, Hamm and Hammerbrook. As in the first RAF attack, they continued down to the factories and docks areas on the Elbe before heading back to England. The northeastern "wedge" of Barmbek, Winterhude and our district, Uhlenhorst, were again spared from the heavy bombing, although a few bombs fell quite close to our house.

It was on this night that the bombing created the first tornado firestorm. It was so fierce that it destroyed large areas of the city and killed an estimated 40,000 people. Our crypt would not have survived a direct or even close bomb hit and the firestorm would have killed us all if it had reached the church. Fortunately, it didn't. The firestorm lasted for about three hours, reaching enormous heights and unprecedented temperatures. By using many incendiary bombs and blowing out roofs, doors and windows with exposive bombs, the buildings were turned into vast chimneys drawing air in at the bottom and out through the roof, burning everything inside. Fires joined together to produce vast infernoes that nothing could survive in. The flames sucked oxygen out of bunkers and cellars. Many people were found in cellars afterwards, apparently unharmed: they had died of asphyxiation or carbon monoxide poisoning. Thousands of other people were burnt to death in the shelters. In these circumstances, estimates of how many people died was based on collecting and counting the skulls. There was no way they could be identified. This gruesome work was assigned to prisoners from the Neuengamme concentration camp which was a slave-labour camp situated in the marsh-lands about 19 km east of Hamburg. Many people were also buried alive under the rubble that night. The heat from the firestorm was so intense that, in many areas, tarmac on the roads melted and caught fire. People's shoes got stuck in it and their feet were burnt to stumps. Some people managed to reach one of the many canals running through the city and survived the firestorm by jumping into the water, although many then drowned. Over 2,300 tons of bombs were dropped on Hamburg in that raid. We had miraculously survived the bombing as we were on the fringe of the main attack zone. Our shelter was about 3 km from the centre of the firestorm.

In the morning we crept warily out of the crypt. The air was hot and smokey. We could see the red glow of fire and the smoke coming from buildings in the distance. We walked back to our home in Zimmerstraße which was untouched. Our mother put us to bed. During the night in the crypt we had dozed a little but we had not slept properly as we were too frightened. Later, when she woke us, my mother noticed that I had developed a pronounced squint in my left eye and I also had a high temperature. My eyes had been perfectly normal before that night: the squint was presumably caused by the shock of the bombs going off, creating a trauma we had all suffered in the crypt. The bombing destruction had cut off the utilities: there was no water, electricity or gas available in the apartment. However, we had a solid-fuel stove. Our mother used it to warm up some previously cooked stew she had stored in the kitchen cupboard. She invited a neighbour from upstairs, a young lady she was friendly with, to come down and join us in this simple meal. As we were eating we wondered what would happen next. Our mother was thinking what can we do? Would the bombers return? Was there anywhere safe in Hamburg?

In the early afternoon, a woman assisting in the evacuation of Hamburg, came to the door. She told our mother that (under an edict by Gauleiter Kaufmann) all women and children *must* leave the city this very day. Dolly packed a suitcase with clothes, toiletries and a few items of cutlery (which the woman had advised her to take). Fortunately our mother had the foresight to take her British passport. She also took a scarf with a Union Jack on it and a very useful silk scarf which had been printed on both sides with a map of Germany. (It was made in England and may have been intended for British invasion forces: I still have it.) On that day, 28 July 1943, approximately 1.2 million people out of a pre-war population of nearly 2 million, were evacuated from Hamburg, Germany's second largest city. The logistics of this evacuation were unprecedented, especially as the railway system had been highly damaged by bombs and many roads were blocked by blast holes and rubble.

Adam Hamelmann somehow managed to find transport to rejoin his ship, the Cap Arcona which was docked in Gotenhafen (Gdynia) in the Baltic Sea. His wife (my aunt) Trudel Hamelmann was also among the evacuees. She spent four days on trains travelling down to Lustadt in the Pfalz region to stay with Adam's aunt and uncle (Eva and Heinrich Völker). Everywhere was packed with people struggling to get out of Hamburg. Her son Walter had to stay in Hamburg as he had just been recruited into the army (at the age of 16). Trudel had not heard from him and did not know where he was but she hoped he wasn't on flak duty in Hamburg, which was often the job of young recruits. In fact, the poor lad *had* been assigned to flak duty. Opa Max wanted to stay in Hamburg and protect their house from fire-bombs, which he did (and as he had done before, Chapter 3). Their apartment house was still standing intact then, although it was somewhat nearer the centre of the firestorm than ours was. The Americans had carried out their daylight raids which Trudel hoped would help to persuade him to leave. She did not want him to risk his life trying to protect their house. It would be very difficult for him to stay there anyway as water, gas and electricity had been cut-off in most of Hamburg. Food supplies had been disrupted, how would he cope? With bombing going on day and night, Trudel hadn't slept properly for days and was looking forward to being far away in peaceful rural Lustadt. To her enormous relief, Opa Max *did* join her soon after she got there. Our father, Maximilian, was still in the Lüneburg army camp. We didn't get to see him during this traumatic period.

Amazingly, despite the destruction, a lot of the city's bureaucracy was still functioning to organize the evacuation. Later that afternoon, a lorry came to our street. My mother with a small pushchair, a suitcase and us two young children, climbed into it. Several other people joined us until the lorry was full. We were driven by a circuitous route out of Hamburg avoiding, as much as possible, the fire-storm damage. Eventually we reached Zarrentin, a small town about 60 km east of Hamburg. It was already evening when we got there. We were led into a room full of bunks with men, women and children all together. Everyone was confused and anxious. There was a doctor on duty so Dolly asked him to take a look at me. He examined my squint and advised my mother to take me to an eye specialist when we got to our destination, wherever and whenever that might be. He also gave me something to get my temperature down.

During that night (29/30 July 1943) while we were in Zarrentin, the third Gomorrah attack started. This took place despite the fact that most of Hamburg already lay as a burning ruin and a million people had been evacuated from the city. It seemed that Sir Arthur Harris would not be satisfied until every last house had been destroyed. A group of 777 RAF bombers crossed the North Sea, assembled into a formation and then attacked the city from the north. They bombed the small area of Hamburg which had been left mostly undamaged, including parts of the districts of Wandsbek, Barmbek, Eimsbüttel, Winterhude and our lovely home district of Uhlenhorst. Trudel and Adam's beautiful house in Uhlenhorster Weg was hit by incendiary bombs and was completely burnt out. The bombers hit areas that were still burning. Some streets like the Hamburger Straße, Mundsburger Damm etc, were also destroyed, with not a single house left standing. The large shopping store, Karstadthaus, was bombed and collapsed, trapping nearly 2,000 people sheltering in its cellars. Most of them were rescued to safety but several hundred died. They were either burnt to death, asphyxiated or buried alive. During this third Gomorrah operation, many thousand more people were added to the death toll.

The third RAF operation suffered as many plane losses as the previous two operations combined. Somehow the Luftwaffe had learnt, to some extent, how to cope with the radar-blocking chaff and could spot some planes through the radar fog. They adopted new, more aggressive, fighter tactics. Sir Arthur Harris was keen to finish the destruction of Hamburg so that not one brick was left on top of another. The weather had turned unfavourable so a fourth attack was postponed a couple of times. A giant thunderstorm had developed over north-western Germany on the night of 2/3 August but Sir Arthur Harris thought it would disperse. He gave the go-ahead for another Gomorrah attack. The conditions turned out to be disastrous for the RAF. The planes suffered lightning strikes, Ice formed on their wings and engines which caused several of them to crash. Others lost their bearings. The Luftwaffe attacked and shot down many RAF planes. A few bombers finally reached Hamburg. The destruction had been so great that there was actually very little left for them to do anyway. From the RAF point of view, this last operation should not have taken place: it was a self-inflicted disaster.

Operation Gomorrah consisted of four RAF night-time bombing raids, two USAAF daytime raids and many night-time Mosquito "nuisance" raids to make sure that no one got much sleep during that 11 day period. At the end of Operation Gomorrah, over half of all the homes in Hamburg had been destroyed. An estimated 45,000 people had lost their lives. Mass trench graves were dug in the form of a cross in Hamburg's large green park-like Ohlsdorf Cemetary. Each trench was filled with over 10,000 bodies or shrunken charred remains. Reporting to Berlin, Hamburg's Gauleiter Kaufmann, described the situation as a catastrophe on an unprecedented scale. He urgently invited

Hitler to come to Hamburg and see the damage for himself but the Führer refused. The task of providing transport for refugees (including our families) and of feeding and housing the remaining inhabitants was unimaginably difficult. Operation Gomorrah was judged to be the most destructive assault in the history of aerial warfare up to that time. It was later called the "Hiroshima of Germany". There was a greater weight of bombs dropped on Hamburg in one night than were dropped on London throughout the whole of the second world war.

We were certainly evacuated in the nick of time. We learnt later that our apartment house was hit by an incendiary bomb the following night (29th July) after we had left. It was completely burnt out, although the outer shell of the building remained intact. Everything we possessed had gone. All our books, letters and photographs were burnt. Our remaining clothes, furniture, pictures, china and glasses were all destroyed. Our few toys were lost, apart from my sister's doll which she had taken with her and my little brown teddy bear which I hugged close to me. He kept me safe. It had been a beautiful apartment! The same day that we left (28 July 1943), my aunt Else Koschel, her husband Richard and their daughter Rosi also fled from Hamburg. Else wrote the following two letters to Werner a short time after the bombing. They give a graphic record of the effect the Gomorrah attacks had on the citizens of Hamburg and the massive damage they caused:

(9. 8. 1943): We have lost our lovely home in Hamburg, which a couple of hours before, we had been so proud of. Your beautiful home was also taken by the flames, as Opa has written. How will your mother cope with this terrible news? After the second attack, Richard and two friends had bravely protected their house from incendiary bombs and flying, burning debris. But the second attack was so terrible that one had no other thought than to get out of Hamburg as soon as possible and as far away as

possible. The images of our flight from Hamburg were so gruesome that they stop your heart from the shock. Those who escaped alive from this Hell were very lucky. And that is now the sad truth, we little people, as we receive one blow after another, can do nothing but wait and wait again for what Fate has in store for us. But one thing I must live to see is that this Hell, which has come over us poor Hamburgers, will be more gruesome and terrible over those who thought of and carried out this horror. I need to see this this happen so that I do not lose my faith in Justice.

When Werner had returned from Russia, severely wounded, Else wrote to him again:

(27. 9. 1943): I thank you very much for your long letter from Lyck, (in East Prussia, now Elk in Poland). You cannot believe what a stone fell from my heart when your letter arrived. We have had such dreadful misery this year and if something awful had happened to you, I could not have borne it. I do hope that, as you write, you are making a good recovery and that you can stay out of Russia. In good time you will become a smart, healthy young fellow again. We have lived through so much this year, which whole generations before us have never experienced, but so gruesome and shocking that, if we have peaceful times again, we will ask ourselves how could we have endured something so dreadful? It has taken me months, at least from the outside, to recover my mental equilibrium after receiving the hardest blow a mother can have. (This refers to her son Edgar, see Chapter 7).

I remember very clearly, as we were on our way to the Gänsemarkt (goose market), you said to me, 'How peaceful it all is here, the people here know nothing about how it is at the Front. They all need to go there.' And then Hell came over Hamburg. We got through the first attack together, but the second attack (with the firestorm) over-night from Tuesday to Wednesday (27 – 28 July) destroyed our reason, drove us all insane. We knew only one thing clearly: we couldn't protect our houses. There was only one thing to do: we must get out of Hamburg to stay alive, as fast as our legs can carry us. After your mother (Trudel) had gone, I implored Walter and Opa Max to follow her to Mrs Schröder in Ahrensburg (a town not far north of Hamburg). Then Richard and I fled. We were to be evacuated on a lorry to Bergedorf. The driver went via Berliner Tor and, I believe, Hoheluft or Hamm, I don't know anymore where, I only know that I saw burning and destroyed houses on both sides of the road. I didn't know where we were. We saw heaps of partly naked bodies, heaps of burnt bodies lying on the streets and lorry loads of burnt S.D. men in the middle of the road. (S.D. men were the Social Democrats who largely comprised the working class in Hamburg, in bitter opposition to the Nazis.) Then I prayed to dear God not to let me go mad. I pressed both my hands into my eyes to stop me seeing this horrible vision. Then we reached streets that were completely blocked by ruins and the driver had to turn around and go back again. We went past glowing ruins, past the shock of so many collapsed houses and standing ruins until, half-dead, we arrived with our fellow passengers at Harburg station (south of Hamburg).

We had at any rate escaped Hell but the fear of air attacks is, and remains for ever, in the blood. My dear Werner, Rosi and I were in Hamburg last week to fetch some clothes to take to safety. Of course we went to see your house and stood in front of it. What can one say? My heart stopped for a minute and I could not take it in.

Below, in the cellar, lay a giant pile of rubble and above, four naked outer walls of the house. And that was all that remained of the home that your mother and father created with so much love and taste for twenty years! Only a couple of hours and everything, everything was a pile of waste and ruins. Rosi and I were devastated. Rosi moaned over and over again that this was not believable, inconceivable! We wandered further through the streets, Mundsburger Damm, Hamburger Straße, Winterhuder Weg. All ruins, ruins, ruins! It is horrible, as you say, Werner. It would be unbearable if Mamma, Papa or Walter had been buried in the rubble. It is truly amazing that we all came out of it alive. This fact, which we are truly happy about, must be the counterweight to all the other sorrows we bear.

This turned out to be the wartime Diaspora of our Family. The Hamelmanns were split up again with Werner going back to Russia, Adam to his ship, the Cap Arcona, and Trudel going to relatives in Lustadt in the Pfalz region of Germany. Opa joined her shortly after. Walter, as a new recruit, had to stay in Hamburg on flak duty. The Koschels, Richard, Else and Rosi went to their second home in Krakau. We Barths were already split up, Maximilian was in the army in the Lüneburg camp, while our mother Dolly, Annemarie and I were refugees in Zarrentin waiting to find shelter somewhere. It was an anxious and miserable time for everyone: what does the future hold for us all now?

The name Gomorrah, used for the attack on Hamburg, comes from the Biblical story of God's destruction of two towns on the plain of the dead sea: Sodom and Gomorrah. He sent fire and brimstone to punish the inhabitants for their wicked deeds. The story was probably derived from the devastating earthquake that occurred in that region around 2,000 BCE.

Gomorrah

Gomorrah, and Gomorrah, and Gomorrah,
Dark clouds of planes attack from dusk to dawn.
Now all the people who were living, laughing,
Drinking coffee in green parks by the Alster,
Have fled this Hanseatic Hamburg,
Or been vernichtet, burnt to dusty death.
Eight hundred bombers flying low
And raining down their bombs and fire
Until the last home was burnt out,
Leaving standing just an empty shell.
Brothers killing brothers: acts of violence
Full of Sound and Fury, signifyng nothing.

(Based on lines from Shakespeare's
Macbeth: Tomorrow, and tomorrow,…)

Gomorrah, und Gomorrah, und Gomorrah,
Dunkle Flugzeugwolken greifen an von Abendrot bis
    Morgengrauen.
Menschen, die gerade noch feierten, lachten,
Und Kaffe tranken im grünen Alsterpark,
Sind nun aus ihre Hansestadt verbannt
Oder zu staubigem Tode verbrannt.
Achthundert niedrig fliegende Bomber liessen
Ihr Feuer und ihre Bomben niederregnen,
Bis von dem letzten Haus, ausgebrannt,
Verlassen nur eine leere Hülle stand.
Brüder ermordeten Brüder: Gewalttaten
Voller Klang und Wut, die nichts bedeuten.

(Translation by Bettina Melchers,
daughter of Klaus Melchers)

Chapter Seven

The Koschels in Krakau

---

*The earth together with its surrounding waters must
in fact have such a shape as its shadow reveals, for it
eclipses the moon with the arc of a perfect circle.*
NICOLAUS COPERNICUS 1473 – 1543, KRAKÓW UNIVERSITY.

When the Koschels, Richard, Else and Rosi, fled from
Hamburg at the end of July 1943 during Operation
Gomorrah, they went to Krakau (Kraków) in Poland. They had
rented a second home there since 1940 because of Richard's
business interests.

As a boy in the early 1900s, Richard had gone with his family
to Blumenau, Santa Catarina, in Brazil and grew up there. He
worked for various companies, based in Hamburg, trading with
Brazil, included a magnesium mining company. (It's an interesting
thought that the magnesium from his mine could have been sold
to Britain and found its way into the incendiary bombs that were
dropped by the RAF on Hamburg during the war.) Richard
met Else in Brazil in the 1910s, probably in Rio. She had gone
there in her teens as an au pair (Chapter 1). During her voyage

to Brazil she met a ship's steward called Adam Hamelmann. It was on the long voyage that he fell in love with her but she did not return his feelings. He persisted and kept in touch with her and her family in Hamburg. On one visit to the family, he met Trudel, Else's younger sister. The two sisters were both good looking, intelligent girls. Somehow, he transferred his wooing to Trudel and this time, hit the jackpot. Adam later became Chief Steward on the luxury liner the Cap Arcona which was launched in Hamburg in 1927. It carried passengers between Hamburg and various ports in South America.

Richard was still working in Brazil. His friendship with Else continued and blossomed until in 1919 he proposed marriage and she accepted. He suggested they should have the wedding in Blumenau because his family were still living there and he knew it well from his boyhood. Blumenau is a city about 800 km south of Rio on the Itajai river, some 40 km from the coast. It was founded by German settlers and is famous for its beer brewery and German style half-timbered houses. Richard, who always seemed to have plenty of money, booked the most luxurious hotel there for the wedding. Else had her own room to prepare for the happy event. The hotel was filled with guests invited to the celebrations and it was used for the reception. It was planned to be a splendid event but it was almost a disaster. Richard had been on a trek in the jungle for several weeks with his brother and ran into unexpected difficulties. Else was getting nervous because there was no sign of them. Much to her relief, they arrived by car late on the day before the wedding. Richard needed time to get the mosquitos and twigs out of his hair and get smartened up. He and Else were married on 25 August 1919. They had both a church and a civil ceremony. After a short honeymoon in Blumenau, they went to Rio to live in Richard's apartment.

From 1920 until the outbreak of war, Richard worked for a company called Alex Kalkmann & Co. It imported various technical goods from Hamburg to Brazil. He made regular trips between Hamburg and Rio during the next two decades and, with his keen business acumen, rose in the company. When Alex Kalkmann died, Richard took over and the company continued to prosper. Less than two years after their marriage, Else gave birth to her first baby, a girl, in March 1921 in Hamburg. They named her Rose Marie but she was always known as Rosi. She grew up in Hamburg, did reasonably well at school and developed into a bright, beautiful and spirited young woman. Else's second child, a boy, was born in September 1922, also in Hamburg. They called him Edgar and he grew up into a handsome and clever young man. Rosi and Edgar were close siblings and spent much of their time together. Edgar was the young lad (14 years old) who presented my mother with a bouquet of flowers from the Koschels on her wedding day in Hamburg but, as they had not been introduced, she assumed he was a delivery boy (Chapter 2). She noted then that he had "beautiful long eyelashes".

In August 1939 the Non-Aggression Pact between Hitler and Stalin was signed. They had agreed to carve up Poland between them. Soon after, German forces marched into Poland. Parts of former East Prussia, including the capital, Königsberg, were retaken by the Reich. The western part of Poland became the Warthegau and the south-western province (formerly Silesia) became a German colony ruled by the "General Gouvernement". The Eastern half of Poland was taken and occupied by the Russians. By the summer of 1940, Poland, as an autonomous country, had entirely ceased to exist! Grossdeutsches Reich (Great Germany) came into existence. (With this name, I think Hitler was emulating Great Britain which, as a world empire, he had always envied and aspired to supercede.)

The General Government established its headquarters in Krakau. In November 1939 there were mass arrests of academics who were sent to concentration camps. The University of Krakau was closed indefinitely. As a centre of learning in Europe, Krakau was amongst the most ancient and finest, boasting of Nicolaus Copernicus (1473 – 1543) whose astronomical observations and calculations led him to propose a heliocentric model of the solar system.

Hitler put his former private lawyer, Hans Frank, in charge as Gauleiter, although he had no experience of administration. Hitler seemed to choose and dismiss his gauleiters on whimsical likes and dislikes. It was no wonder that the Nazi Reich was filled with greedy incompetent yes-men. Hans Frank was also deeply corrupt: he stole and plundered Polish treasures and then went on lavish spending sprees. He restored and refurbished rooms in Wawel Castle and ran his government from there. Frank's extravagant display of wealth led to him being called King of Poland and his domain being dubbed "Frankreich" (a pun, as it is the German for "France"). He spent a lot of money sponsoring the arts: painters, writers and musicians. He developed a full programme of concerts, opera and exhibitions of art works put on in Krakau. There were also lavish feasts for some occasion, anniversary or other. Resident Germans and Polish fellow travellers enjoyed the cultural highlights during Frank's rule. Meanwhile, Krakau's Jewish population, which had notably been there since mediaeval times, was reduced from 68,000 to almost zero. They were deported to Auschwitz and Belzec concentration camps and murdered.

The main task set for the new government was to modernize and mechanize Polish agriculture in order to increase food production and thus release surplus labour for the war effort. This created new business opportunities. It was also encouraged by the Nazi government as part of the "Germanization" of Poland. In 1940 Richard Koschel's firm (Alex Kalkmann & Co) concluded a common-interest agreement with the firm of Willi Fuhrhop. This firm had obtained a Four Year Framework agreement under the Reich's Economic Ministry which conferred approval for running their business in Krakau under the General

Government. This was an opportunity for Richard to take his family there and set up home. They moved into an apartment in Lagardegasse, a fine street in Krakau. The joint firm ran under the name of Willi Fuhrhop and worked to their mutual interest until September 1942, when the partners fell out. The partnership was dissolved and Richard had to look for new opportunities on his own.

Richard was an astute businessman. He created an agricultural trading cooperative called "Rolnik", the Polish word for "Farmer". It dealt in modern agricultural machinery, farm implements and supplies. He also opened a second business called "Hammonia" (from the mediaeval female symbol of Hamburg) which consisted of a large shop in Krakau selling fabrics, cloth and materials. His businesses thrived and the Koschels were prosperous and enjoyed a good life there. They could also afford to keep their home in Hamburg (Zimmerstraße 35) where they also spent considerable periods of time. Richard was always noted for having the knack of making money.

Koschel's "Rolnik" shop in Krakau, 1940/1.

Richard Koschel was unusual in not being recruited into the armed forces. In 1941 he was already 50 years old but it was not his age that kept him out of the Wehrmacht. In Germany all male inhabitants were registered for military service when they reached the age of 18. It was his good fortune that he was still living in Brazil when he reached that critical age, so the German Wehrmacht had no record of him. His civilian status was not questioned because men who were powerful or important to the regime were also not called up. He did not disillusion people who wondered about his status: he preferred to stay out of the army.

When Else, Rosi and Edgar moved to Krakau, they enjoyed the lovely places around them. Krakau is a fascinating and beautiful city set on a bend of the river Vistula. Wawel Royal Castle is situated on the hill overlooking the river. There are remnants of the walls which surrounded the ancient city. The space outside these walls has been turned into a circle of parkland called Planty Park, with paths, trees, flowerbeds, ponds and friendly cafes. It houses a statue of the famous astronomer, Nicolaus Copernicus.

Richard, Else, Rosi & Edgar Koschel in Krakau

The city was also noted for its very old Jewish Quarter. It has, what is claimed to be, the largest city square in Europe: Rynek Glowny. Part of the square is occupied by a long building which was the ancient cloth market and now contains restaurants and shops. Cars are prohibited but horse-drawn carriages give rides to the tourists. Facing the square is a 14th Century Gothic Church, St Mary's Basilica and all around it there are beautiful shops and cafes. Else and Rosi bought themselves the latest suits and dresses there, as their photographs of around 1940 – 1943 show. Ladies' hats were an essential fashion item then and they certainly made the most of them.

In the summer on sunny days they spent leisure time at the large public swimming pool which was a favourite place for people to meet. On one side of its length it had a cafe with tables and chairs, leading to a large lawn for people to sunbathe and chat. On the other side of the pool there were rows of tiered seating, as in a Roman arena. This was built for people to watch competitions or displays of swimming and diving. In Rosi's photo collection, there are many pictures of Else, Rosi and their friends enjoying the sun in 1942 when she was 21. The pool had a 10 metre high diving board. There is a wonderful shot of her and Edgar in perfect synchrony diving from this board. The photographs show that Edgar and Rosi were very fond of each other. Most of the young men In the pictures are in bathing trunks but a few unfortunates are in uniform, enjoying a short break before having to get back to the war.

In the winter the Koschels went skiing at Zakopane which

Rosi and Edgar Koschel in Krakau swimming pool, 1942

has a wonderful ski resort in the foothills of the Tatras Mountains, south of Krakau. The views from the tops of the mountains are breath-taking. Rosi, a keen and somewhat reckless skier, enjoyed meeting with her friends there. The Tatras are also lovely in the summer. The family went there for walks and picnics in the Alpine-like flowering meadows. They sometimes made use of a car, borrowed or hired, for their visits to Zakopane and other interesting places. Else could drive though Richard never learnt.

Edgar was called up into the Luftwaffe (German Air Force) in early 1942, when he was 19. Werner got a letter from him (25. 5.1942) saying that he was not being sent to Africa as expected but would be trained as a pilot at the flying school in Linz (Austria) some time soon. He went there for a couple of months, completed the course and was then transferred to occupied France. There he flew as an observer in Heinkel 111 bombers. These were the reliable work-horse planes used by the Luftwaffe throughout the whole of the war. They were powered by two Junckers inverted V12 piston engines and held a crew of five. Each plane was fitted with five defensive machine guns, including one in the observation gondola beneath its belly. It was relatively slow, top speed 436 km/h (270 mph) which was its downfall in the Battle of Britain. Edgar continued his training in France and in the summer of 1942 was given leave: he rejoined his family in Krakau. The weather was warm and sunny so they spent a lot of time at the swimming baths

*Edgar in a Heinkel 111
as an observer, 1942*

where they met other friends and enjoyed themselves. At the end of his leave he went back to his squadron.

A few months later, Edgar was on a training flight as an observer, in the region of Dijon, near the village of Allerey. Two Heinkel 111s were in the air at the same time. They flew rather too near one another and were low to the ground. At one moment they became too close together. One of the planes did a turn to avoid the other, lost control and hit a poplar tree. The plane disintegrated and all five men on board were killed, including Edgar. It was the 12th of December 1942; he was just 20 years old. His mother, Else, received the news of her son's death on Christmas Eve, usually a big festive occasion for Germans. She threw herself onto her bed and wept for hours. She suffered grief for her loss for many years afterwards. The Luftwaffe sent Edgar's belongings back to his parents, included a fob watch bearing the marks of his violent crash. Werner sent the sad news in a letter (17.1.1943) to his mother, Trudel (Else's sister).

*

The Koschels, like the Hamelmanns and our family, the Barths, were all in Hamburg when Operation Gomorrah started in late July 1943 (Chapter 6). The Koschels left after the second attack and returned to their home in Krakau. Rosi was engaged to be married to Günter Uttermann who was in the Luftwaffe in France. Preparations for their wedding in Krakau had already been made so, despite the terrible destruction of Hamburg they had witnessed, the wedding went ahead. They were married in a Register Office on 28 August 1943. Else wrote to Werner:

(27.9.1943): We come now to Rosi's wedding which, as you know, was celebrated for three whole days! Some of the wedding guests, the youngsters of course, came on Friday and only left on the Sunday evening, when the

Wedding of Rosi and Günter Uttermann, August 1943.

happy couple departed. We were drunk for three days and then sober again, but it was wonderful. Photos were taken over and over again and in the next few days, Rosi will send you some.

Else then encouraged Werner to come to Krakau. (This letter was sent at the end of September 1943 when Werner had been wounded in Russia and was recuperating in hospital: Chapter 8). Else said that they had plenty of room, lots of good food and always Schnaps. They could go out to lively cafes, listen to good music and have long conversations. She wished him, above all, a good recovery.

Before Rosi met him, Günter Uttermann had been sent to Russia but he was far enough away from the Front to have missed the worst of the fighting. After Russia he was posted to France in 1940 as a Communication Officer in the Luftwaffe, in charge of rigging telegraph and telephone lines. Life was much more congenial there as it was a military occupation rather than a shooting war. From his photo album in August 1940, he seemed to be having a wonderful holiday on the beaches of Normandy, near Houlgate and Mont St Michel. He and his comrades are often seen in beachwear exercising to keep fit or just sitting round a table discussing telephone line rigging (or how beautiful the girls on the beach are?). He was pictured frolicking in the waves with a young lady called Monique, in St Pair-sur-Mer. He wrote on the back of one of the photos, "Bathing is twice as nice when it's with the loveliest girl in the resort." War wasn't all "Iron and Blood" (Bismarck). If you were lucky, it was an all-expenses-paid beach holiday – with a few fireworks.

Chapter Eight

Werner Wounded in Russia

---

*Man kann es kaum für möglich halten, dass derartige
Zerstörungen möglich sind, wenn man es nicht mit eigenen
Augen sehen würde. Ja, der Traum von unserem,
schönen Hamburg ist aus.*

WERNER HAMELMANN, LETTER TO HIS FATHER (22.10.1943)

*(One can hardly believe that such destruction is possible if
I had not seen it with my own eyes. Yes, the dream of our
beautiful Hamburg is gone.)*

In Chapter 6, we left Werner at Hamburg Hauptbahnhof on the 25th of July 1943 wishing farewell to his father Adam. He reluctantly took the train to Berlin, the first leg of a long journey that would take him back to Russia. That morning had been the end of the first phase of the Operation Gomorrah attack on Hamburg. He thus missed the second two major Gomorrah air attacks. When he reached Berlin, he was put on a train with other troops heading to Russia. The following day they arrived in Insterburg (now Chernyakhovsk) in former East Prussia, east of the former capital Königsberg (now Kaliningrad, in a Russian enclave). The next leg of the journey took them to Tauroggen (Taurage) in Lithuania, a mere 80 km in a day. It then took them another two days to get to the Russian border, where they stayed for two more days. At some point in his journey, the train stopped at a station. Werner got out of the train because he was anxious to get the latest news about the bombing in Hamburg. He was looking for someone to ask in the station buildings when suddenly, without a warning whistle, the train moved off. He ran after it waving and shouting but couldn't catch up with it. All his military and personal luggage, everything, was in the train. He was a radio operator so this included all the heavy electrical equipment which was in use in the 1940s.

Werner loved telling stories about his war years. He told them so well, even if he was the fall-guy. He described his horror at seeing the train gathering speed as he ran down the platform shouting and waving. All his precious radio and other army equipment were hurtling away from him. He could have been court-martialled for careless neglect, but years later he had us all laughing at his vivid description of "The Day the Train Went off Without Me".

Werner managed to get on another train later that day and continued his journey. He finally reached his destination, Tosno in Russia, in a baggage train on 2nd August 1943. Tosno is about 60 km south of Leningrad on the main road and railway line to Moscow. A tributary of the river Neva runs through it. Due to its strategic position, it had been occupied by German forces since August 1941. It was a quiet place where the terrible sounds of war in Leningrad could not be heard. He rejoined his old Wehrmacht unit there.

Werner reported for duty to Feldwebel (sergeant-major) Sondmann, who was known as the "mother" of the company. He welcomed Werner back to the camp and said, "We have been waiting for you. Why are you so late getting here? We need you and your radio urgently. Where *is* your equipment?" Werner had to explain how the train had gone off without him so he had no idea where his radio equipment had got to. Sondmann suddenly became a very stern "mother" and things looked bad for Werner. However, he made enquiries and, with Wehrmacht efficiency, all Werner's baggage and radio equipment were traced and delivered to the camp six days later. Werner tested the circuitry of his radio to check all was in order. (Months later all was forgiven it seems. Werner sent a parcel of goodies to the company from Hamburg. The Feldwebel replied with a letter (10.9.1943) of thanks and good wishes for his recovery from Sondmann and his comrades.)

The following day Werner was given weapons for a military operation. Because of his late arrival at the camp, he had to catch up with the rest of the troop, who had already advanced to Lake Ladoga, the large lake east of Leningrad. When he arrived, they told him of their previous attack. On that same evening, they got ready and set off at 7 pm. He slung the heavy radio equipment over his shoulder and, with his battery colleague, joined the others. (Radio equipment in those days required two men: one to carry the actual radio and the other to carry the heavy lead/acid battery needed to power it.) With a tank leading the way, a group of them headed along the Neva river bank towards Leningrad. They moved steadily ahead for a few miles. Suddenly, without any warning, there was a crack from the front. Werner had been shot. "It was worse than being hit on the head by a grenade." The bullet went right through the middle of his radio, through his right shoulder, thus missing his heart, and out again. He fell backwards into a shell crater and was unable to move for about two hours. His colleague with the battery pack rushed to help him. He saw Werner lying there motionless, saw the damaged radio and a lot of blood everywhere and thought he looked dead. He ran off to get help. Other colleagues came and realized he was, fortunately, still alive. They put Werner on a stretcher and took him back to a dressing station. After some basic tending of the wound, it was obvious that he needed treatment by a surgeon. His shoulder joint and lung had suffered severe injury.

Werner was dispatched by train through the night to a Feldlazarett (military field hospital). He had time to reflect: this was his first day of military action after his leave in Hamburg. He had started at 7 pm and by 9 pm he was already wounded and out of action. Two hours could be the shortest spell of action by any soldier in this war. As a radio operator he had to carry his heavy equipment on his shoulder, so being wounded there meant he could no longer operate. It was in the perfect place for a wound to take him out of the war. Werner was always the optimist. He thought, "What luck, I am out of it." This was only true, of course, if he survived!

The train travelled on through the night. In the morning he arrived at Krasnogwardeisk, now called Gatchina, about 50 km south of Leningrad. He was taken to the field hospital there. It was August, the weather was warm and sunny. This was a blessing for there were many wounded and sick people waiting there in the open, near the buildings and tents. He took his place in the queue. Eventually, when his turn came, the doctor took Werner's shirt off and examined him. There was such a lot of blood, it was difficult to see the wound. The doctor told him that they had run out of anaesthetics so there would be some pain. He was taken into the surgery for the operation. The surgeon first cut out a small section of his shoulder that already looked gangrenous and then sewed up the large hole from both sides. Werner was left to recuperate in a tent. There were other patients lying in there with him, some of whom were Russian. Werner had learnt some Russian during his time there: he got into conversation with them. They talked about their families and passed round photos of their wives and children. He had a packet of cigarettes in his pocket which he took out to share with them but unfortunately they were now wet, bloodstained and useless. Werner was only 19 so the Russians were mostly older than him. They seemed, understandably, nervous about being treated by German doctors. But "enemies", ordered to shoot each other in a war can recognize and treat each other as fellow human beings off the battlefield – though this was not in the ruthless philosophy of Nazism.

Werner had not received any letters from home for a while because he had been moving about so much. But soon after this, letters started getting through to him again. Werner learnt for the first time that his family had left Hamburg after the second Gomorrah attack. He was always so worried when he heard on the wireless news that more attacks had taken place and that most of Hamburg was now lying in ruins. He kept urging his family to leave. "Don't worry about the houses, they can be rebuilt, but you must find safety." It was an enormous relief when he found out that they had left Hamburg and were now with his father's uncle and aunt in Lustadt in the Pfalz region. "Don't worry about me, I am feeling fine. I am being well looked after and, for the first time for a very long while, I am being allowed to live without war" (15.8.1943). He was lying in bed most of the time and let his thoughts wander. He killed time by reading a lot. Writing was still very difficult because he could hardly bend his right arm. Werner found that his uniform, recently so nice and new was now torn, dirty, wet and bloody. He took it off. "A pity, but that's war!" But he was happy, predicting that he would be out of the fighting for a long time. "It was really Hell there! So few of us survived the battle."

Werner wrote to his mother (3.9.1943) that after a two day direct journey in a Bulgarian hospital train, he had arrived in Lyck in East Prussia (which is now Elk in Poland). It was then four weeks since he had been shot in the shoulder. He was overjoyed to be back in Germany! His 20th birthday was two months away. Werner was quite near Gotenhafen where his father worked on the former cruise ship Cap Arcona but his mother was much further away. He would love to have her visit but he tells her to wait as he doesn't know how long he will stay in Lyck. Adam writes him a long letter from the ship (7.9.1943). He was shocked to hear about his wounds but was very pleased that it had taken him out of the "Hell in the East. It will be months before you are fit enough to be sent to the Front again and now you are in safe protection which will ease your mother's and my mind." He tells Werner about the destruction of Hamburg with over one million people evacuated. He explains what happened to all the family and hopes to visit him in Lyck on the 18th September, if he is still there then. Adam made the visit and they went for a walk together. He thinks they will release Werner from the hospital soon. However, his recuperation took another six weeks.

During this time there were many letters between Werner and his parents and quite a few parcels containing writing paper, hard boiled eggs, money and cigarettes. Adam warns him not to smoke too much and certainly not into his wounded lung. (Is it possible to control which lung you breathe into?) Some of his lung was lost in the shot and the surgery. Adam warns Werner that smoking can lead to tuberculosis of the lung (no mention of cancer in those days). He has set up a scheme with the head waiter of the Station Hotel in Lyck. Adam sends him cigarettes (a universal currency in those days) and the waiter looks after Werner. "Go there to eat, especially on Sundays and Tuesdays and he will give you 18 Marks and look after you well." Werner obviously takes up this chance and enjoys the food and wine they serve him. His new uniform has arrived, foreshadowing his dreaded return to the battle-field.

Werner had accumulated 12 days' leave and wanted to go to Hamburg via Gotenhafen where he could see his father. However, army regulations won't let him: he has to go via Berlin. Perhaps he could visit his father on the way back? He departed at 22 hrs on 19th October 1943 and arrived in Hamburg the following evening. He was about to go on the S-bahn (city railway) when there was an air-raid warning and he had to take shelter in a cellar for two hours. Finally he reached the home of their friends, Else and Bruno Krüger at 2 am. He sent a telegram to his mother in Lustadt. She arrived in Hamburg the following day. After all these months of war and destruction and worry about who was still alive, they were so pleased to see one another again. It was such a pity that Adam couldn't be there as well. Werner thought that, when he got his next convalescence leave, he could visit them again.

The next day Werner went, for the first time, into the city. He was not only shocked by the terrible destruction but also surprised at the lively hustle and bustle in the centre. It was hardly believable how people, despite the destruction, carried on with their daily business and amusements. Werner writes to his father:

(22.10.1943): Things were much the same as before, as if the Hamburgers are saying, 'Now, first Justice!' So many people are here again, I think it is more lively than it used to be. In contrast, other parts of the city are dead and empty. One can hardly believe that such destruction is possible if I had not seen it with my own eyes. The dream of our beautiful Hamburg is gone. We must hope that the day of reconstruction will come very soon and, above all, that Hamburg is spared any more such attacks.

Werner got back to Lyck on the 1st of November 1943 to continue his convalescence. His release was delayed several times but he points out to his mother that he wins this way. His time in hospital is taken off his time in the war, but the length of his leave from the army still remains the same. The delay means he has sadly missed being in Hamburg for his mother's birthday and will probably miss being there for his own (both in November). More importantly though, he very much wants to get leave over the Christmas period. His father Adam on the Cap Arcona is making preparations for the festive season. He has bought a Christmas present for Trudel: a silver fox-fur coat for 1,500 Marks from a police officer who is on leave from Norway. There was a choice from five fur coats and they are the very best quality, much better than from a German fox-farm, he thinks.

As the month wears on, "release fever" breaks out in the hospital. Werner finally got a spell of leave in Hamburg again, including a 48 hour stop at Gotenhafen to see his father on the ship. On the afternoon of 20 Nov 1943, his 20th birthday, Werner caught a train to Königsberg. It was a terrible journey because the train had no heating. Also, he had spent the previous afternoon enjoying himself at a wedding reception so he was very tired and probably a bit hung-over. He had to wait there for three hours and then caught the train to Berlin at midnight. He planned to change trains at Dirschau for Gotenhafen. The Berlin train was heated and he got a nice comfortable corner seat. He snuggled down and, of course, fell asleep immediately. He missed his stop and didn't wake up until it was light and Berlin was only a few minutes away. He was shocked and upset but it was too late to go back to Gotenhafen.

Werner wrote, "It was Fate that a stupid sleep caused me to miss something I had been looking forward to for so long." He arrived in Hamburg and got to the Krüger's house early in the afternoon. Werner was so happy to be with his mother, brother and friends again: a joyous reunion. The following Monday he was transferred to the Military camp at Oldenburg, Holstein and soon after that he was given the two weeks leave of absence he had built up. He spent a wonderful Christmas period in Hamburg among family and friends. But this was not the end of the Wehrmacht service demanded of him by the Führer.

Chapter Nine

Refugees in Bavaria, 1943

At the end of Chapter 6, my mother Dolly, sister Annemarie and I had been evacuated from Hamburg after the second Operation Gomorrah bombing attack during the night of 27/28 July 1943. We had been taken by lorry to Zarrentin, a small town east of Hamburg, where we were looked after, along with very many other nervous and frightened refugees. A doctor had examined my squint which had been triggered by the trauma of the bombing and given me an antibiotic (presumably sulphonamide) to reduce my fever. We then slept the night in bunk beds in the crowded room.

The following morning we were taken to the station. The railway infrastructure in and around Hamburg had been badly damaged by the bombing, which was why we had to leave the city in lorries. Zarrentin's railway lines were still intact, connecting to Lübeck and Kiel to the north-west and to Berlin in the south-east. As refugees, we could travel wherever we wanted without a ticket. Our mother knew that Trudel Hamelmann, my aunt, had relations in south-west Germany in the Pfalz region and thought that she might be able to make contact. So we boarded a south-bound train. The first stop was Wittenburg where we were offered sandwiches by volunteers standing on the platform. The train stopped again somewhere in the coutryside that night. We could see lights in the distance. However our train had no lights on at all, presumably to avoid being seen by enemy aircraft. After many hours, we reached a small town where teenagers stood on the platforms, again offering help. We were taken to a house where we slept in shared beds for the night. It all seemed so well organized. Next morning they gave us breakfast and then took us back to the station.

The train standing at the platform was already absolutely packed. My pushchair was accidently squashed in the crush of people boarding the train. We set off again, stopping at Beyreuth and then Regensburg in Lower Bavaria. The train continued on south through Bavaria. Finally we stopped again at the station in the little town of Marklkofen. It was a fine sunny day. We got out of the train to stretch our legs and looked around at the picturesque Bavarian houses. We were given lunch in the hotel across the street. Someone announced that if any of us would like to stay in this district, accommodation could be found for us. It was a beautiful part of Germany and we had suffered two days of crowded train travelling, so our mother opted to stay. We were taken by bus to the adjacent town of Frontenhausen.

When we got there, we were lined up in the school yard to be inspected by potential hosts. People from the town came along and looked at us as though we were some sort of strange exhibits. One women said to her husband, "*they* don't look too bad, we'll take them". He was a coal merchant which oddly, but luckily for him, kept him out of the army. We followed them to their house, feeling tired after all the travelling. We were given the use of just one small room at the top of the house, for the three of us. It had a cot, bed, washstand, chair and a table. They had a downstairs sitting room where their little daughter played. I wanted to play with her but when I did, she cried and so her mother sent me off upstairs again. To me it seemed unfair, why shouldn't I be allowed to play? I was only two and a half years old. The mother then made it clear that we were not welcome downstairs.

Every day after breakfast, we had to leave the house and were only allowed back in the evening. We went to the school for our meals. The catering was run on a voluntary help basis. Our mother, Dolly, helped out by peeling potatoes, cooking and serving meals. On fine days we went off into the lovely countryside around Frontenhausen but when it was wet, we had to go to the library or some other public space: our hosts wouldn't let us stay in the house. At weekends they often went to visit relatives so we were then, and only then, allowed to use their kitchen and eat there. Our life was very restricted. The Bavarians generally were not very welcoming to the refugee Hamburgers. As in England, there was a noticeable north-south divide in Germany.

In early July 1943, about a month before we were bombed out of Hamburg, our father Maximilian was moved from his comfortable posting in Nantes in France. We don't know why this was. He may have been sending us too many parcels or been drinking too much French wine or brandy (it was no secret that he was fond of alcohol). On the other hand, he spoke French pretty well and may have been fraternizing and drinking with the locals in the bars (combining two sins). Whatever it was, he was thrown into military jail for a short spell and then sent to the army base at Lüneburg for some shooting practice. He had been living a soft life in France for two years and the Wehrmacht needed some more canon-fodder on the eastern front. Max was sent to Russia, to the battle front at Leningrad, as a rifleman in September 1943. It was a hell on earth for everyone involved. The siege of Leningrad had been going on for two gruelling years of bloodshed in which over a million people had been slaughtered (Chapter 4). He just missed being there at the same time as his nephew, Werner Hamelmann, who had been posted there the previous month in early August 1943. But Werner had just returned to Germany to recuperate after being shot through the lung and shoulder (Chapter 8).

Maximilian didn't stay long in Russia either: he suffered a similar fate to Werner. In early October, Max was shot and seriously wounded. He was sent to a field hospital where he was treated and after a period of recovery, was sent back to Germany. He was admitted into the reserve field hospital in Rothenburg near Hanover. News of this reached us in Frontenhausen. My mother went to see him in the hospital. She found that he had a serious bullet wound, he was very thin and she feared he might not survive. She helped to feed him and put her nursing skills to good use there but she couldn't stay long. We, her children, had been left in the hands of another refugee in Frontenhausen who was looking after us for a few days until Dolly returned.

Max spent many weeks in the hospital for his wounds to heal and to recover his weight. He was sufficiently well to be discharged briefly from hospital in November 1943. He was given leave to meet us in Westhausen, Baden-Württemberg, which is not far from Frontenhausen. He looked a lot thinner and older than when we had last seen him. We hugged and kissed him, our dear Papa! It was a very emotional reunion. We wanted to know what he had been doing in the army. When was he going to come and live with us again? He told our mother of his horrifying time in Russia and his close brush with death but not us children, of course. Our short reunion was just for one day. We went back to Frontenhausen and Max went back to the hospital. When he was fully fit again, he was posted to the Horst Wessel Barracks in Hamburg. He was still in the army but after his near-death experience, at the age of 43, he was put on fire-watch and security duties. Despite the continued sporadic bombing of Hamburg, this was now a much safer option than being at the Russian Front. He was, of course, much happier to be back in his home city.

Meanwhile, back in Frontenhausen, our mother discovered that many other refugees were being housed in the splendid

Hotel Röhrl. That seemed a much better option than being confined, as we were, to a single room in a house with unfriendly hosts. Dolly made enquiries and discovered that a room had just become vacant in the hotel. She went to the Town Hall and asked whether we could have it. Luckily, they said yes. As refugees, we were given vouchers to pay for food and accommodation. So, after staying only a few weeks with the coal merchant and his wife, we were able to move out. In the hotel we were given two rooms on the top floor. This gave us more freedom. Annemarie and I had more space to play in and we no longer had to go out all day, whatever the weather. We could also use the public rooms in the hotel and talk to other refugees and locals there. Our lives suddenly became more open and varied.

When it was time to wash the clothes, we had to gather fuel because the allocation of coal for this was not sufficient. Our mother took us and a small four-wheeled box-cart out into the woods. Usually other children came with us too: it became a fun day out. We spent all afternoon in the lovely countryside, playing games and finding interesting plants, insects and mushrooms. We gathered pieces of dead wood and fir cones and put them into a sack. When it was full, Dolly loaded it into the cart and trundled it back to the hotel. On the way back, two or three children, including me sometimes, were given a ride on top which was great fun. The fuel was used in an open stove in the hotel to heat water for the washing.

We lived in Frontenhausen for about a year. At some time during our stay there, I caught measles which turned out to be very severe. I was taken to a Catholic Hospital where the nuns looked after me. My body was covered from head to foot in spots and it was so bad that I could barely open my eyes or eat anything. My mother, a trained nurse, also looked after me and was very worried that I might not survive. Measles can sometimes be lethal to under five year-olds (I was three). The nuns were very kind and looked after me very well. Fortunately I recovered, with no scars to show for it.

Our father Maximilian was still in the Horst Wessel Barracks in Hamburg, on patrol duty, fire-fighting and general policing of the ruined city. He kept in touch with his nephew Walter who was then 17 and on flak (anti-aircraft gun) duty in Hamburg. In early August 1944, Max arranged for us to visit him in Hamburg. We got there by train, a long slow journey which was exhausting. We were very pleased to see our Papa again. Having got there, our mother would have preferred that we should all stay together in Hamburg. However, life was still very difficult after the destruction. Air raids still occurred, although they were small and sporadic. There was no repeat of the Gomorrah fire-storm and carpet bombing we had escaped from in July 1943. Even so, Maximilian thought we would be safer in our quiet little town in Bavaria than in Hamburg: he made no move to bring us back together as a family. Max wrote to Adam and Trudel Hamelmann shortly after our visit:

(17.8.1944) Annemarie will be 6 years old on the 25th of this month. I'll send her a nice little card. The little lass is so sweeeeet! I would have loved to have her here with me a few times during my stay in Heide. A very special girl!! Have you heard from Werner? I was so happy to hear that, up to the 10th of July, he had not been sent back to the battle front. My thoughts are very much with him and I wish, from my whole heart, that he stays healthy.

At that time Max had not heard that Werner had been shot through his right lung and was recuperating in hospital (previous chapter).

The situation was starting to get difficult for us in Frontenhausen. In June 1944, American bombers, mostly B24s, started bombing raids on the oil refineries and industrial areas of Vienna, which included the Heinkel aircraft factory. This continued throughout the summer months. Refugees from Vienna and other parts of Austria started arriving in Bavaria. By August 1944 the problem was getting acute and pressure was put onto refugees from northern Germany, like us, to find billets further north. Priority was being given to the Austrian refugees: we needed to find a new home again.

Chapter Ten

Werner in Denmark and Norway

While we were in Frontenhausen in Bavaria having an uneventful but thankfully, bomb-free life, Werner had been sent to Tosno in Russia. He had been shot through the lung and shoulder and brought back to Germany for surgery and recuperation. In early January he was sent to the military camp in Oldenburg, Holstein, having had Christmas in Hamburg but missing the New year's Eve celebrations. He wrote, "In the Wehrmacht you have to give up some of your freedoms."

Werner was recruited into the news company because of his radio training. He was amazed and delighted to meet up with two old comrades from his radio group in Russia. They all prayed for the good luck not to be sent to Russia again and one of these friends had a scheme to achieve that. He was an assistant to a film and radio producing group. Because of his expertise and adaptability, he was needed in Germany, which was how he had managed to stay out of the hot war for a year. He was scheduled to go to Hamburg for an interpreter's course the following week and suggested that Werner might apply to go with him. He jumped at the chance: he and his colleague received the necessary three days leave. First, Werner had to take a written exam, which he found difficult. Next he needed to sit an oral exam in Hamburg. Werner thought the exams didn't go well for him but at least they had enjoyed themselves there. He feared the worst however, that if he didn't pass, he would be sent back to Russia.

Werner did not get to see his mother in Hamburg because, at the time, she was on the Cap Arcona with his father, Adam. He requested and was given leave to see them both. He was packed and ready to go when his leave was cancelled and to his great surprise, he was sent to Camp Fallingbostel on Lüneburg Heath instead. No reason was given to him for this move. Other soldiers arrived in dribs and drabs. Finally a group had been assembled. They were told that they were forming an important new radio team and Werner was promoted to Radio Team Leader! He was amazed and delighted. It was a great position that he had never dreamed of getting. Looking back, he realised that his exam results must have been much better than he thought. The new group stayed in Fallingbostel for a few months training, but their mission was still kept secret. Werner was so pleased that he wrote to his parents, "Fate has been good to me. I actually *like* being in the army! Everything is excellent." This, of course, was being in the army without doing any fighting. In the middle of March 1944, the regiment started to move out. In Flensburg on the border of Denmark, Werner sent a card to his father saying they were on their way north, reported in a letter (20.3.1944).

In Aarhus, Denmark, they stopped for a few days. Werner was keen to convert his newly received Krone into Schlagsahne (whipped cream) and all that goes with it (coffee and cakes, eggs and bacon, pretty well everything). He had time to look up some of the relations on our grandmother's side (Ane Marie Mikkelsen) who came from Klovborg. He went to see Hroar Fog, who had lost his wife, Aunty Johanne (Ane Marie's sister) five months earlier due to a stroke (exactly as had happened to Ane Marie). There was also his son, Asbjørn Fog, in Aarhus-

Risskov. When Werner, by arrangement, fetched him from the church, despite the long years gone by, Asbjørn immediately recognised Werner. They were close family members who were put, against their will, onto opposing sides of the war. Denmark had been occupied by the Wehrmacht early after the start of the war and was largely self-governing with little interference from their fellow "Aryan" masters. But nevertheless, they were a subject nation.

Werner and Asbjørn were very pleased to see each other again. Werner expressed an intense longing (Sehnsucht) for the liberation of Denmark and an end to the war. On the last day of their stop in Aarhus, Werner visited him again. He telephoned Asbjørn who fetched him from the station and took him back to his house. There they drank coffee and had a long chat: Asbjørn spoke very good German. They talked about his family, his wife Ragnhild and their six children, all boys. He also talked about his time in Africa. Asbjørn was a church missionary in Nigeria and had left just a few days before the German invasion with very little money and few possessions. When he got back to Denmark, all he could afford was a small house with a few sticks of furniture. He was studying for exams to continue his vocation as a minister in the Church and earn his living. He was well known in the Danish Sudan Mission and had written a book entitled *Five Negro Priests*.

The regiment spent six days in Aarhus. They then boarded a freighter which took them on a 30 hour sea voyage to Oslo. Unfortunately they didn't have much time to look around as they had to unload all their equipment from the ship. Even though Oslo was actually built on an American pattern, it looked to them to have a typical European face. They could easily believe themselves to be in Germany. German was being widely spoken and they saw Nazi propaganda posters everywhere. Similarly, there were few things to buy in the shops. The main difference was that "everything smelt of fish". The Norwegians hadn't had any meat for three years.

After two days, the regiment travelled by train to a town not far from Oslo. Werner names it only as "B" in his letters but clues suggest this fits with it being Bergen. They moved into their quarters in a fine old building, with central heating and hot water. They had nice comfortable rooms, excellent food and beautiful surroundings. The town was quite small but very pleasant. Werner thanks God that he has come here and "not to the accursed Russia again. It seems like being on holiday here. At the moment the snow is still piled high but when summer comes, it will be lovely." As summer came the landscape went green and the sun warmed the earth and their faces. There was nothing much to do except some marching and shooting practice. Letters came and went but there was very little news. A few parcels with cigarettes and cakes arrived. In return, Werner sent parcels to his mother containing writing paper and baking powder which seemed to be in very short supply in Germany. Furs were also available in Norway and not expensive. Werner complains that "Walter never seems to write, he is just a lazy trumpet player." He also writes that he has not had much time to write letters. This is unconvincing: Werner always made time when interesting things were happening. He longed for the "Entscheidung" (the final decision) to be made: the final hammer blow to end the war.

The 6th of June 1944 (D-day) came and went. Surprisingly, there was no reaction at all from Werner or his family. Was the news being suppressed by the propaganda machine? Perhaps it was made to seem unimportant, or were they just playing "wait and see what happens"? Werner had been sent to Norway to protect the "Atlantic Wall" that Hitler had established from Narvik down to Bayonne. As part of this wall, Bergen and Trondheim had U-boat bases. Werner enjoyed himself in Bergen: it was a nice town, lovely scenery and no fighting, yet. However, the Normandy landings were about to change all that. One week after D-day (13.6.1944) he sent a letter to his mother in Hamburg telling her that they had done a lot of marching around the parade ground to get themselves fit again. "I am still enjoying myself here despite the (Allied) invasion. Don't worry about the sudden developments, it will all turn out well and the end of the war won't be far away." On the 25th June, Werner wrote to his father that the Allied Invasion had started. "We will wait to see how things develop, it will go badly for them." The same day, in a letter to his mother, he advises her to go to the Pfalz. "It is safer there than in Hamburg which is still being attacked. You always see things darker than they really are. We *will* succeed and the more optimistic you are about this, the easier it is to achieve."

As if to show how relaxed he was about the progress of the war, Werner had been to Oslo a few days earlier to see a performance of Mozart's *Marriage of Figaro*. It was a long time since he had been to an opera and he was absolutely inspired by it. "This has been the best three months of my time in the army." It was a well-deserved holiday.

Chapter Eleven

A Wehrmacht Division moves to Normandy

---

*Den ganzen Marsch über sahen wir ununterbrochen V1
über uns hinwegheulen. Es war einfach phantastisch,
besonders bei Nacht wo man schon aus weiter Ferne die
Apparate heranbrausen hört, wie ein schwerer LKW aus
nächster Nähe, man sieht jedoch nur den Feuerschweif.*

WERNER HAMELMANN 10.7.1944

(During the whole march we saw an unbroken stream
of V1s howling over us. It was simply fantastic,
especially
at night when one could hear from a great distance
the buzzing sound, like a heavy lorry close by,
however, one sees only the fiery tail.)

The Germans had been caught on the hop. They had been fooled by fake intelligence that Norway would be used for the Allied invasion and so the Wehrmacht kept many more troops there than they needed. In fact, they needed very few. They decided now, rather late, to send the whole Division ("Armee" in German, about 10,000 men) with all its armaments and equipment, from Norway to Normandy. The first move was to Oslo where they spent two days loading their armaments and equipment onto a ship which then took them back to Aarhus in Denmark. In the one day stop there, Werner took his chance to have a good meal. He thought it might be his last for quite a while.

All the men and equipment were transferred into ten long modern trains all of which had very good facilities. They started the long journey south to Normandy. The train of trains travelled only at night to reduce the chance of being spotted by reconaissance planes. On Saturday 24th of June 1944, Werner's train rolled slowly through Hamburg, over the Dammtor Bridge which crosses the Alster right in the middle of the city. To his regret, he only had time to write a quick postcard to his family before they were off again. "It made my heart bleed not to see you all", he wrote. There was no time to say hello or perhaps goodbye to his family. They had a difficult task ahead of them: to open a new front and stop the advance of the invading troops in Normandy.

The trains continued on and before long, they were "in a foreign land" again (the Netherlands). They travelled south through Holland and Belgium keeping close to the coast and making many stops, during which they had the chance to talk to the local people. Werner's school French came in useful. He wrote to his father a rather strange letter:

(1.7.1944): However, at this moment there is something to be understood here (one can speak openly and honestly): France is dead and the bombing terror takes daily worse forms here, as in Germany. Just as the first impression of this country does not match my preconceptions, so the whole journey we have just made seems fantastic and unique, especially in this never ending time for making military decisions. It seems to me that there is a somewhat mysterious attitude being taken by the locals *against* England here, from what we have heard so far. But the most important thing for me is that this time, I was not sent to Russia again! I am writing this first letter by candle-light in a train carriage and I hope the second one will follow shortly."

When they reached Brugge in Belgium, the train went very slowly, making as little noise as possible so that it wouldn't be heard by the planes flying above. During their whole journey thus far, they were fortunate not to have been bombed. As night came, the soldiers took their blankets and stretched out on the bunks or on floor pads and tried to sleep. It was very quiet outside, there was absolute darkness and stillness apart from the repetitive rumble of the wheels. Suddenly there was a noise "like many bombs exploding at once". The train came to a jerky halt. No one knew what was happening, but it soon became clear: a train travelling north on the wrong track had crashed into the first of their trains going south. The engines and carriages at the crash site were piled up "as high as a house" and many soldiers were dead or injured. It was very dark and at first, only a few people realized what had happened. "Soldiers ran around like frantic ants." Gradually order was restored and the officers commanded the soldiers to assemble with their kit, by the tracks, in ranks. They announced that there had been an accident further up the line but "we mustn't let the Führer down. We will continue now … on foot! " Werner wryly observed, "We were following the German custom of arriving too late."

They had to unload all their equipment from the trains. Then they set off south, in platoons of men. Werner was wondering, as always, when they were going to get their next meal. They plodded on for many hours through the countryside and small towns. Apart from the crunch of boots, all was quiet. But suddenly they heard a very loud noise: it sounded like a heavy lorry driving close by. They looked around but couldn't see a thing, so after a shocked pause, the company marched on. Later, they heard the sound again but this time they could see a fiery tail and recognized it as a rocket. It was flying at an "outrageous speed!" It was a V-1 rocket, designed and built in Peenemünde. It had a pulsejet engine which, unlike modern jets, was fired by a spark plug at 50 times a second! This gave it the characteristic buzzing sound and hence the nickname "buzz bomb". The V stood for Vergeltungswaffen (retaliation weapons).

One week after the D-Day landings the Wermacht was provoked to retaliate and used the rockets for the first time. They were launched from several sites in Belgium and France. V-1 rockets were directed mostly at London but fewer than a third of them actually hit their targets. There were various reasons for this, including the existence of a double agent in London. He falsely reported that the V-1s had landed on targets significantly beyond their actual hit sites. Consequently, the Germans reduced the range setting so that the V-1s then fell short of their targets, missing areas of housing. The flight control of these weapons was totally novel (but they seem primitive by today's computer standards). However, the V-1s that did hit houses in London caused a lot of casualties and damage.

The columns of troops marched on, covering about 120 km in four days. This wasn't easy, especially after the relatively soft life they had been living in Norway. There were frequent flights of V-1 rockets throughout the night. They were fired at night-time to reduce the chance of enemy planes spotting the launch sites which were usually hidden in woodland. The sight of these rockets in the darkness was fantastic. Each one gave the soldiers a thrill and raised their spirits. They could imagine what effect they would be having in England. Werner had at one time taken an interest in the V-2 rocket which was more advanced than the V-1. He thought the V-2s could become the Entscheidungs Waffen (decisive weapons) in the war.

As they went through towns and villages during the day they got their second shock of the journey: they were able to buy all sorts of foods, including butter, eggs, cherries strawberries and meat and it was all so cheap! "We were utterly amazed and thought we were in paradise." Werner corrected his earlier assumption that France was dead, made as they were going through miserable empty villages. "I was deceived." Soon after that, they reached their destination camp and felt they really had reached heaven. There were tents in the grounds of a chateau and a lot of good food to eat. The intention was that they would wait for the battle front to reach them. "The front is far away and it should take a long time to get here because our soldiers have already managed to bring the strong invading enemy to a halt. Although, this monstrously delays an already long war." Werner thought that the Normandy Landings would turn out to be a failure like the disastrous "Dieppe Raid" two years earlier (Chapter 4).

They had a lot of work to do, often late into the night. They constructed defensive barriers and bunkers to block any invading allied forces, if they should reach that far north. During the course of this work, Werner injured his right arm somehow, the one which had been affected by the bullet through his right shoulder in Russia in August 1943. He was given leave from heavy duties and allotted the use of a motorbike. He doesn't explain what his brief was but he travelled around, visiting local towns and villages. He found they were peaceful and undamaged by bombs. The people had not fled and were consequently not resentful, unlike the Norwegians. His French was good enough for him to speak to and understand them, so he learnt a lot about their views of the war. He found life there more congenial than in Norway, "as long as there is no fighting".

Werner started studying again. He writes to his father (25.7.1944) that he is getting only two or three hours sleep a night. The course he was following would lead to an officer's rank (R.O.B.) as Troop Leader of the radio news group, which would be installed in a radio-train. He hoped to go to War School in Germany in September. He enjoyed travelling through France in the lovely weather and seemed overwhelmed by the availabilty of good food. Some days later he didn't have to walk or go by motorbike great distances any more as he was given access to a car with a driver. He was so pleased that he had been in Fallingbostel where his training had begun. He had seen so many places this year (1944), in Norway, Denmark, Holland, Belgium and now France. He wanted to spend more time in France when the war was over.

During this time, V-1 rockets could constantly be heard at night in the distance. They were still being fired towards England. He thought they would act as a deterrent to bombs getting through to them here in France. He believed they had not long to wait before victory would be achieved. "Our enemies here and also in Russia are days from their end. We must believe firmly in victory and an orderly peace." He adds that "the worst thing is that the war is getting ever closer to the Koschels in Krakow. If they return soon to Germany it would be especially important for Rosi and her baby." He has news of the death of a good friend of his in Holland. "This war brings nothing but grief and sorrow."

Werner sent a letter to his parents on the 31 July 1944 from somewhere north-east of the Normandy invasion zone. After four weeks of waiting, he was overjoyed to receive a letter from them. He had been sending long reports to them of what he had seen, done and most importantly it seems, eaten! He is now in charge of the News Room. He thanks them for all the parcels they have sent over the weeks but points out that he has actually received only a very small fraction of what they have apparently sent. So perhaps it would be better to stop as he has plenty of food, but maybe the parcels of cigarettes could continue? His view of the war continues to be optimistic. He writes to his parents:

(31.7.1944): I have little fear that the Eastern front will be rapidly retaken. When we bring the Russians to a stop with a massive fire-storm, as in 1917, we will have won the war. I think we can do it and not only there but here in the west as well. What we really have is not known to our enemies: the amazing large-scale operation of our V-1 rockets. These unique pilot-less aircraft, like missiles, flying away in all directions over us, make the air groan like an earthquake. It brings us courage. We have a hard task to carry it through but I am certain that the end of the war is not far away. The Führer has escaped unharmed from an assassination attempt again: this must be a supernatural sign. It has strengthened my belief in a good future. I only hope you will escape the effects of the war in northern Germany.

Werner's belief in the "supernatural" and his optimism seem to me to be misplaced. He is referring here to the attempt by Claus von Stauffenberg to assassinate Hitler in his headquarters in East Prussia. An opportunity occurred when von Stauffenberg was ordered to make a presentation to Hitler at a briefing in his Wolfsschanze (Wolf's Lair) Headquarters on 20 July 1944. Stauffenberg was the leader of a group of anti-Nazis who wanted to assassinate Hitler and bring back a democratic government. They thought that, ideally, they would need to kill Himmler and Göring at the same time, so that the Nazi Party would be decapitated. They planned to seize power then and make peace proposals to the Western Allies as soon as possible. Unfortunately Himmler and Göring were not invited to this briefing, but time was running out. Many previous assassination plans had already been abandoned because of last minute changed circumstances. So von Stauffenberg decided to use this opportunity to make an attempt on the life of Hitler at least and hope that the rest would follow.

He was flown from Berlin to Rastenberg, close to the Wolfsschanze headquarters. His aide-de-camp, Haeften, met him there carrying two briefcases, each containing a bomb. Under the guise of changing his shirt because of the hot weather, Stauffenberg primed one of the bombs but ran out of time to do the second because the time of the meeting had suddenly been changed from 13:00 to 12:30. He carried the primed bomb in his briefcase into the conference room and placed it by his seat, near to Hitler's, under the large heavy oak map table. He was told that the time for his presentation had been delayed so he excused himself from the room "to make a phone call to a colleague in Berlin for further information relevant to the briefing". Haeften was outside with a car: they waited together. There was a big explosion in the map room. They immediately made their carefully planned escape, not waiting to see if Hitler had actually been killed. More than 20 people were injured in the bomb-blast, three of whom later died, but Hitler, protected from the main blast by a big oak table leg, was injured but survived. The repercussions of the failed coup on the plotters were swift, ruthless and gruesome. Werner took Hitler's survival as a supernatural sign but, if there *were* forces at work, they were evil: Hitler seemed to have the "luck of the devil"!

*

After a long period in comfort in the grounds of the chateau, Werner's company had been waiting for the invading forces to arrive. Then orders came through to go south and "fight them on the beaches" or wherever the enemy had advanced to. The company moved down the coast and arrived at one of the beaches the Americans had landed on. Right there on the shore were a number of lead chests which had presumably been there since the invasion about eight weeks earlier. The troops shot off the padlocks and looked inside. They were full of ships biscuits. The

Americans obviously valued cookies so much that they were part of the essential invasion supplies. The Germans were hungry after their long march, so they helped themselves to handfuls of biscuits and ate them standing there on the beach. Right behind the lead chests was a prisoner of war camp. An American firm called MOS was loading scrap iron onto lorries. They were stripping down valuable materials and taking them to Caen to be shipped to the USA. Scrap iron would be needed to rebuild American industry. They were cashing in before the war was over.

The German troops pulled south to Argentan and Le Mans but central control by the Wehrmacht seemed to be failing. The troops fragmented into smaller groups. They took to hiding in houses and cellars in the villages. Werner was now in just a small squad of men who organized themselves. They reached an empty farmhouse and looked around. They made themselves comfortable and waited to see what would happen. Four chickens were clucking and running around in the hen coop. The men had not eaten for a long time so they caught the chickens and prepared them for cooking in the kitchen. They couldn't find any vegetables so they just roasted the hens. However, they did find some Calvados but it was very young and sour. Someone went down into the cellar and found some mature Calvados which was very good. They realized they could not afford to get drunk or they might be caught unawares by the Allies. So they ate this meal of roast chicken with Calvados and then lay out under the trees in the afternoon sun. It was a never-to-be-forgotten meal. Werner said (on tape), "Fifty years later, the taste is still on my tongue!" They slept for a while and then, as well brought up young men, went back into the kitchen and cleared up.

Werner's squad moved on to a small village where they saw a lorry with about ten packing cases in it. They opened one up. Inside they found, to their amazement, pristine bundles of 100,000 French Franc notes. Unbelievable! They started filling their pockets with the money. More German soldiers came out of cellars and joined in the "Freudenfest", filling their pockets with as much money as they could. Later they found bottles of Cointreau in the lorry which they also stuffed into their uniforms, however they could manage. Another lorry was discovered with more packing cases full of money and Cointreau. How was it possible that so much money and booze should be here in this little village?

Despite this bonanza, Werner had a small practical problem: his socks had disintegrated in the last weeks of marching and hiding. Socks were difficult to get but he knew all about Fusslappen, foot cloths, which were much used in the army in the First World War. You put a small cloth inside your boot, inserted your foot, wrapped the cloth around it and folded it over in a special way. In place of socks, they were comfortable and worked well. He knocked on several doors to no avail. Finally he reached the last farmhouse in the village and knocked. A young woman came to the door and Werner asked, in his best French, if she might let him have a couple of small hand towels. She went back into the house and found some. He was then able to get his feet comfortable again which was more important than all that money and booze in his pockets. The young French woman was left wondering what a German soldier wanted with two small hand towels.

There was a young priest in the village who asked Werner to act as an interpreter for him. He led Werner to his house, sat at his desk and talked about what was happening in the war. But it was just a ruse because, suddenly, he ran out into the street shouting that a German soldier was in his house! There was a commotion, shots were fired, no one was sure by whom, and one of the German soldiers was hit. The situation escalated and the Germans drew back into cellars or wherever they could hide. The priest and Werner went out to look at the soldier who had been shot: they found he was dead.

A British military jeep arrived in the village. The British soldiers showed no anxiety because they had been informed that there were no German troops there. They walked around the middle of the village with their weapons. More British troops arrived. The German officers, who "did everything to 100% or 150% efficiency", had miscalculated how many Allied forces were in the area. They thought their troops could make an armed escape but now they saw that they were heavily outnumbered. The German troops (about 500 men) therefore surrendered. They were led off under guard. With their pockets stuffed with the French Francs and Cointreau, they waddled off: marching was impossible. As they shuffled up the road, everyone tried to hide in the middle of the group. They were directed into a large field. At the entrance they had to give up their weapons in designated piles: rifles here, hand guns over there, etc. A British soldier shouted in a mock German accent, "For you, Fritz, the war is over!"

When that was all done, the Germans sat down in the field and had a good look at the bank notes. 100,000 Francs was an unbelievably high denomination. Then someone spotted that they had no watermarks: they were fake! The German Government had sent them to destabilize the French Franc. The word went round fast, the notes were fake, worthless! They had been millionaires for less than an hour. One soldier stood up and, with a dramatic gesture, threw all his Francs in the air and watched them fluttering down around him. Another one stood up, laughed and threw *his* Francs in the air. Then they all joined in, dancing and scattering the fake money to the wind and laughing. The whole camp was a crowd of jumping, laughing and shouting men in clouds of fluttering, worthless paper. As a compensation, the Cointreau was found to be genuine.

This chapter was another of Werner's stories of the war, captured on tape, which he told so well. I am always left with the wonderful image of the men in the field jumping and laughing: "The Day the Sky was full of Money".

The regular letters home from Werner ceased. As the weeks went by with no news, his mother and father became distraught.

Was he alive or dead? Finally on the 10th of October 1944 they got a short note from him in an Allied prisoner of war camp. He sent his greetings to family and friends hoping they were all safe and sound. "Don't worry about me, I am fine. I would love to hear from everyone. Turn the wireless on to D.R.K." (Deutsche Rundfunk Kriegsgefangenenlager = German Radio for PoW camps). Part of his letter, about where and when he was captured, was redacted. The war had another seven months to run, but for Werner, the war *was* over. His parents were enormously relieved to hear that he was still alive and in the hands of the Allies, not the Russians.

Chapter Twelve

The Koschels Flee from Krakau

"I was 8 years old in the spring of 1945 when my family fled Silesia to escape the Russian Army. On our way we passed through Dresden. A few days later it was firebombed. The fire was so bright that night that one could read a newspaper from the light, though we were many kilometres away."

Günter Blobel, Nobel Prize Winner, 1999.

Towards the end of 1944, the war was turning against the Germans. Richard Koschel learnt that the Red Army had broken through the Wehrmacht's "Eastern Wall" and was moving west. He may have heard this from someone in the General Government headquarters in Krakau. It was not the sort of news broadcast readily by German radio, which had to be all good news from the Nazi perspective. He decided that they must leave the city as soon as they could. He started closing down his businesses which took him several weeks. He told Else and Rosi, who was heavily pregnant, that they needed to get ready to leave. They packed their fine clothes and personal belongings in suitcases. Richard had a significant amount of money in Polish Złotys which would probably be worthless back in Germany. He wondered what he could do with it. He was a keen stamp collector so he had the idea of buying hundreds of sheets of stamps from the post office. He saw them as an investment and packed them in his bag. There is some evidence that a few of his employees decided to leave Krakau with them. They headed north-west in early December 1944.

Hans Frank, the Nazi Gauleiter of the General Government, lowered the swastika flag on Wawel Castle on 17 January 1945 and fled from Krakau in his large bullet-proof Mercedes. He was followed by his henchmen in a convoy of lorries containing the most portable of the valuable items he had accumulated over the five years of his reign. Some of this loot had been stolen from Jewish people when they were arrested and sent to concentration camps. During Frank's rule he had acquired a significant haul of paintings, silverware, clocks, books and objects d'art by these means. He also looted paintings from the National Museum in Warsaw. One item of particular interest was the highly regarded painting "Palace Stairs" by Francesco Guardi. The convoy made its way north-west to Seichau Palace in Lower Silesia, (now Sichów in Poland). This palace and the surrounding estates had previously belonged to Baron Manfred von Richthofen, the famous First World War fighter pilot, the "Red Baron". It held paintings and valuable tapestries collected by the von Richthofen family. One branch of the family had emigrated to Australia and collected unusual aboriginal artworks which were also in the collection.

Gauleiter Frank acquired the palace in 1940. Throughout his time in power he made frequent visits there as a weekend retreat but he also used it to store his stolen treasures. When he and his staff arrived there, the first thing they did was to sort through the government papers and make a bonfire of all the self-incriminating documents i.e those listing his part in the Jewish holocaust and his theft of treasures, etc. According to the staff of the palace, Hans Frank and his group then had a riotous party lasting several days, leaving a chaotic mess of wasted food, broken china, glasses and empty bottles. The plunder Frank had acquired during his time in Krakau included paintings by Leonardo da Vinci, Rembrandt, Dürer, Cranach and the Guardi. Frank and his cohort stayed there for a week and then took his more portable treasures, including the paintings, to his large house in Bavaria. Visitors there were astonished at his collection. Hans Frank didn't have long to enjoy his plundered artwork, however: he was captured by American troops in May 1945. He was handed over to the Nuremberg War Crimes Tribunal and tried in November 1945 alongside other Nazi leaders. He was found guilty of war crimes and hanged in October 1946.

The Koschels had also headed north west through Silesia. Rosi kept a diary of the following year, 1945. Although it has few personal thoughts or descriptions in it, it does contain a record of when and where they went. Their first stop was when they reached Bad Flinsberg (now Swieradow-Zdroj in Poland). This is a beautiful spa town in the spectacular mountains near the border of the Czech Republic. Rosi realized that the birth of her baby was imminent. The fear and stress of the flight from Krakau may have caused the birth to be premature. They had gone to Bad Flinsberg because they knew of the very fine clinic there, built as part of the spa facilities. Rosi was admitted. Very soon after, on 8 December 1944, she gave birth to a baby boy whom she named Klaus. They stayed in Bad Flinsberg for about two months. The stay there gave Rosi time to recover from the birth and for Klaus to develop. (This coincided with the visit of Gauleiter Frank to Seichau Palace, about 60 km east of Bad Flinsberg. Unfortunately, the beautiful palace was burnt down later that year, by Russian troops, it is thought.)

An outbreak of a highly contagious disease (perhaps typhus or dysentary) hit the clinic. All the occupants were ordered "*not to leave, on pain of death*", to prevent its spread. Else argued that, if they stayed there, they would risk catching it, so they crept out secretly in the middle of the night and moved on. Else persuaded an employee to drive a lorry back to Krakau and fetch as much of the stock of goods from Richard's shops as was practicable, including rolls of material from Hammonia. (Klaus remembers seeing rolls of cloth in the store-room of their house in Hamburg after the war and even wearing "Indianer" clothes, i.e. inspired by American Indian styles, made by his mother from these materials.) On the 19th February the Koschels left Bad Flinsberg and headed to Raudnitz (now Roudnice nad Labem, in Czechia) situated on the River Elbe, over 100 km south-west of Bad Flinsberg. The Elbe runs through Hamburg: they were hoping to get there by steamboat via Dresden.

*

Dresden was the capital of Augustus II "the Strong", the Elector of Saxony, who was later also crowned King of Poland in 1697 in Krakau. (He was nicknamed "the Strong" because he could break a horse-shoe by squeezing it in one hand. What is less well known is that he did this trick with horse-shoes that had cracks in them which his viewers could not see.) Augustus was involved in many wars, which he generally lost. What changed his fortune and consequently that of Dresden's, was the discovery of how to make porcelain. This came about by a series of chance events. A man called Johann Böttger, an alchemist in Berlin-Potsdam in 1701, had promised to turn base metal into gold for King Frederick of Prussia. After many years of unsuccessful attempts, his allotted time was almost up. Böttger, knowing the king was famous for his ruthlessness, secretly fled at night and escaped to Dresden. Despite all his failed efforts over the years, he still believed in the ancient myth of producing gold from other metals. He promised to perform the alchemical magic for Augustus. The Elector locked him in a suite of rooms in his castle and provided assistants and all the equipment and ingredients he asked for. After two years of work, there was still not a whisker of any gold.

Augustus threatened Böttger with execution in 1703 but, fortunately for him, the Elector also had an alternative plan: he put Ehrenfried von Tschirnhaus in charge of the project. Tschirnhaus was a proper scientist who didn't believe in mystical alchemy. He had been trying to produce porcelain of the same quality as that imported at great expense from China. No one in Europe had managed to make the hard resilient Chinese porcelain. So Böttger abandoned the fruitless transmutation into gold project and joined in the work of trying to make porcelain. The two men continued with the experiments Tschirnhaus had already started. Tschirnhaus died soon after, probably of dysentery, not knowing that he had got very close to success. Böttger continued the work, using the notes of experiments which had been carefully written up. He finally succeeded using a specific blend of three silicate minerals: quartz, feldspar and kaolin fused together at very high temperatures. Augustus realized that, although mystical alchemy had failed to produce the gold he sought, modern scientific methods had produced "white gold": porcelain. Recognizing the contribution he had made, Augustus released Böttger. He had little time to enjoy his freedom however: he also died soon after, possibly from the effects of the poisonous fumes they had produced in some of their work. Augustus, having got what he wanted, started the manufacture of porcelain in the laboratory rooms. These soon proved to be too small, so he had the equipment moved to Meissen castle where the work could continue on a larger scale, with the process kept very secret from the outside world.

Augustus had always been interested in architecture and had commissioned many architectural plans of buildings. As the money flowed in from Meissen porcelain, he was able to rebuild Dresden in the classical style of the early eighteenth century. It became an extraordinarily beautiful renaissance city known as the German Florence or "Elbflorenz". It was a great European tourist destination and also the sometime home of famous writers, artists and composers such as Caspar David Friedrich, Ibsen, Schumann and Wagner.

The Bombing of Dresden 1945

Why was Dresden, a European architectural and cultural jewel, bombed almost to complete destruction, in the closing stages of the war? It was assumed by most people on both sides of the war that, because the city was such a unique example of classical architecture and there were no major armament factories there, it would not be attacked. What led the Allies to commit the dreadful bombing raid?

There were some strategic reasons because of the railway system there. Since the invention of railways, Dresden had built a large rail network. The Hauptbahnhof (main station) was a beautiful building completed in 1898 just south of the Altstadt. A new bridge had been built to carry rail tracks to the north over the Elbe river. Tracks were also built to towns south, east and west of Dresden until it developed into a major hub of the German railway system. The main north-south and east-west train line axes ran through the city. There were direct lines between Berlin in the north and Munich and Vienna in the south and during the war it was important in connecting the eastern and western Fronts. Large troop movements had shuttled through Dresden during the war. Soldiers were now heading east to confront the Russian advance. The railway through the city was also connected to the concentration camps of Auschwitz and Theresienstadt. Many train-loads of prisoners had tragically passed to their death through this illustrious city.

Also significant to the Allies was the fact that the railway infrastructure was linked to a few industrial sites. In the outskirts of Dresden there were stations and goods yards serving factories and warehouses. Manufacturing sites included the large Zeiss-Ikon works which produced precision optical equipment, especially cameras. The factory had been adapted to supplying components for war machines, including bomb-aiming devices on aircraft. Other factories supplied radar equipment, military components and small items such as bullets. However, there were no factories producing large war machines such as tanks or aircraft. But Dresden's strategic position in this military railway network may have sealed its doom.

The argument against the plan to bomb the city was, of course, its almost unique historical and cultural importance. Another reason was the fact that Dresden happened to be packed with thousands of homeless refugees fleeing west from the Red Army's advance. This included my family, the Koschels, who were travelling through Silesia/Poland heading towards Dresden. The population in the city was very vulnerable because there were few air-raid shelters and no secure bunkers had been built. Gauleiter Mutschmann, used the "Cultural Gem" argument to proclaim, "They are unnecessary, Dresden will never be bombed!" Hypocritically, he had a bunker built for his offices in the city and a second one in the garden of his large private residence.

Cellars under apartment blocks had been prepared as shelters but not reinforced or equipped with air pumps and filters. Door-sized holes had been made in the brick walls between adjacent cellars to create escape options and improve air flow. (These, however, contributed to the firestorm effect, described below.) Dresden's few anti-aircraft guns and searchlights were also thought to be unnecessary: they had been stripped out for use in another German city where the need was deemed to be greater. Tragically for Dresden, they were at this very moment sitting uselessly in a railway goods yard waiting to be shipped out.

In the War Office in London, the proposal to bomb Dresden was put on the table. Dresden was one of the few almost untouched major cities in Germany. Viewed from the British point of view, bombing it would show the Nazis that there was nowhere the Allies could not reach. Destroying the rail network could have a significant effect on the German war effort by disrupting troop movements and damaging the supply factories there. Also, it was thought that bombing it would have a major effect on morale in Germany. These arguments won approval for the attack over the cultural and humanitarian arguments against it. The task of planning a bombing raid on Dresden was given to Air Chief Marshall Arthur "Bomber" Harris, head of Bomber Command. He had a great deal of experience of planning bombing raids including, of course, Operation Gomorrah the destruction of Hamburg, being his "greatest" achievement. It was agreed that the attack on Dresden should go ahead when the weather conditions were forecast to be favourable.

At dusk on the 13th February 1945, the first group of Avro Lancaster bombers took off from England heading for Dresden under the control of Bomber Command. Some of the planes' armour had been stripped out to lighten them so that extra fuel tanks could be fitted for the exceptionally long 2,700 km round-trip journey. In the first attack, a total of 244 bombers set off in altitude layers (to avoid collisions) towards Germany. Dresden had already been subjected to a small number of daylight raids but nothing serious. The weather was clear: they were enjoying an early spring. The city was a sitting duck, visible and undefended, although Bomber Command did not know that then.

At 10 pm the first air-raid sirens started sounding in Dresden. Most people thought this was another of the many false alarms they had heard. It was Shrove Tuesday in the season of carnival, called Fasching in Germany. There was a night of celebrations going on in the streets. Many people were still in costume enjoying themselves, laughing, singing and dancing in the streets. Now they had to hurry home to their cellars: how annoying! Shortly after the sirens started, a squadron of fast

RAF De Havilland Mosquito pathfinders dropped marker flares, green ones to outline the city and then white magnesium flares onto designated targets in the city. Germans called them "Christmas trees" because they floated down on parachutes as a column of pretty lights. But there was nothing festive about these flares. It was only at this point that anyone in Dresden realized that they really were under attack.

The first bombing raid took place soon after the pathfinders had finished. The pilots were surprised to encounter no anti-aircraft fire or night fighters. They efficiently carpet-bombed the old part of the city (Altstadt) and the nearby industrial areas. Heavy bombs blew out doors and windows and incendiary bombs set fire to lofts and attics. Hot air rising in the burning buildings, as in a chimney, sucked strong drafts of air through the shattered doors and windows which increased the intensity of the fires. Other nearby buildings also caught fire until eventually they merged together to produce a perfect firestorm. As the air was sucked out of the buildings by the fires, thousands of people sheltering in their cellars, or in those of the main station, were killed by asphyxiation, carbon monoxide poisoning, by the bomb blasts or being burnt in the flames. The sound and fury of the bombing raid lasted only about 20 minutes. After the bombing had stopped, the "All Clear" sirens were switched on but most of them did not work because the electricity supply had been knocked out in the centre of the city. Some brave souls ventured out and tried to extinguish fires. Dresden's thousand-plus firefighters quickly arrived and did their best but they could not control the intense firestorm in the Altstadt. The day was now, appropriately, Ash Wednesday.

Three hours after the first attack, the second wave came in. This was a group of 525 planes, over twice as many as in the first wave. It flew a different route from the first group to confuse German radar air defences. The timing of the second attack was deliberate: to maximize the death and destruction. After the first attack, soldiers, fire-fighters and medical teams had raced into the city to extinguish fires and help the injured. They thought the bombing had finished. But the second attack then caught and killed these emergency workers and caused further destruction. The incendiary bombs fed the fires already burning and created more tornado firestorms that sucked the oxygen out of cellars and suffocated and burnt the people sheltering there to death. But the second bombing raid did not really have that much to do because the first attack had been so effective. They finished off a few areas in the city and then spread out to the suburbs.

There was a third wave of attacks on Dresden by 431 American B-17s, escorted across Germany by long distance P-51 fighters. They arrived around noon on 14th February, attacking, as always, only in daylight. There was even less for them to do after the RAF's two operations but the Americans had not then received any reports about the "success" of these missions. The weather had become cloudy and, due to radar problems, one squadron of bombers flying too far south saw a city on a river and dropped their bombs. Piling tragedy on tragedy, it turned out to be Prague, capital of the Czech Republic, 120 km south-east of Dresden. Other groups found the right target city, Dresden, but because by then there was thick cloud cover, they bombed fairly randomly over industrial and already flattened city areas. A third squadron attacked a nearby synthetic oil plant: this at least had some military purpose.

Over 25,000 people were killed in the bombing. It was seen by most people as a "terror bombing" for several reasons: Dresden was packed at that moment with helpless refugees fleeing from the Red Army. This greatly increased the death rate. The city was an incomparable architectural masterpiece which was largely destroyed. The military munitions factories that were destroyed did not really have a major effect on the German war machine. The damage to the German railway hub *was* significant but again, only briefly so. The tracks were repaired remarkably quickly by a team from Berlin who specialized in this art. The railway bridge over the Elbe had remained intact, enabling the railway hub to be rapidly restored. The military effect was minimal but the human cost was horrendous.

*

On a visit to former East Germany shortly after the reunification of Germany, in the summer of 1990, Annemarie and I, with our spouses, Colin and Jane, visited Dresden. We were having a meal in a pub and were overheard speaking English. A man came over to us and started berating us with tears and shouts about the terrible bombing of Dresden by the RAF in which he had lost friends and members of his family. He said "50,000 people had been killed: blown up, asphyxiated or burnt to death in the firestorm". We replied, in German, that we totally sympathized with his torment and anger: we too had been bombed out of our home in Hamburg in 1943. We agreed with him that the bombing of Dresden was militarily unnecessary and was a war crime. He was stunned: we all became silent and grieved together.

Jane and I revisited Dresden on holiday in September 2008. The city had been neglected during the communist era: the regime had no interest in the German aristocracy or their buildings. Following the reunification of Germany, Dresden started its restoration. The Elector's castle, which had been left after the bombing with just single walls standing in some places, had been largely rebuilt. Other city buildings and parks were restored to their original splendour. But one building above all others had been shamefully left as a ruin by the East German regime: the Frauenkirche.

The magnificent Frauenkirche, was an absolute masterpiece of renaissance architecture. It was designed by the city's architect Georg Bähr and built between 1726 and 1743. It had a large central dome, 96 metres high, with a crowning lantern. The altar and pulpit were positioned beneath it in the centre of

Palace wall in Dresden, 2008

the church with the congregation surrounding them. It had a highly-regarded organ on which J.S. Bach gave a recital in 1736, during the construction period. The Frauenkiche was heavily bombed in the raid of 13 February 1945 but its construction was so resiliently strong that it held up for two days after the attack, before finally collapsing into a large heap of rubble. The communist regime left it like that.

After German reunification, the population urged the city's rulers to rebuild the Frauenkirche (rather than putting in a proposed car park). Local volunteers salvaged and catalogued pieces of rubble and put them into a store. Money for the restoration was raised world-wide from various sources. Günter Blobel (quoted in this chapter's sub-heading) organized a restoration fund and contributed his Nobel prize money (US$ 1 million) to the project. The original architects' drawings were used for the rebuilding. By the use of photographs and 3D computer graphics, conserved pieces of rubble were mapped into the rebuilding, to be inserted into their original positions as near as possible. The charred and blackened

Dresden Frauenkirche, 2008

stones were deliberately left dark so that they would stand out against the new stones. In this way, the building became both a reconstruction and also a monument to the destruction of the original building. Inside, it was as impressively beautiful and acoustically rich as the original.

The Luftwaffe bombed and destroyed Coventry Cathedral earlier in the war, in November 1940. Coventry was faced with a similar dilemma of reconstruction. It did it in a very different way, with the building of a new cathedal alongside the old ruins.

During our holiday we also visited the Grünes Gewölbe Art Museum established by Augustus the Strong in 1723. It occupies eight rooms of Dresden Castle and contains his amazing collection of precious works of art. Three of the rooms were destroyed by the bombing but the collection had fortunately been moved to the Königstein Fortress in 1938 when war seemed likely. Our guide told us the story of the discovery of making porcelain by Böttger and Tschirnhaus in the castle, as related above.

*

By 20 February 1945, six days after the bombing of Dresden, the Koschels reached Raudnitz which is on the Elbe about 70 km upstream from the city. From there they had hoped to go by boat to Hamburg through Dresden. They had heard the terrible news about the bombing raids and destruction there. If they had set off a week earlier, they would have been in the city and could have been caught in the bombing, as so many others were. The destruction in Dresden blocked the passage of any large boats on the Elbe: road bridges had been destroyed and building debris littered the river. Their plans were delayed, so they stayed in Raudnitz until 17 March hoping that the passage might be reopened. However, this did not happen so they went back to Wigandstahl (now Pobiedna, Poland) the village immediately adjacent to Bad Flinsberg, for four days. After that they went on to Prague and spent a week in that lovely city, which had also been bombed, but fortunately not heavily, by the "lost" American B-17 squadron.

The news came through to them that the Elbe in Dresden was open to boats again. So on 9 April they returned to Raudnitz and embarked on the steamboat "Weimar". During the voyage, Else suffered a fall and broke a rib. They arrived in Dresden on 12 April but unfortunately the information they had been given was wrong. The river was still blocked: large boats could not get through. They decided not to stay there, which was lucky because the RAF had not finished their bombing. Rosi notes in her diary that there was an attack on the Albert docks in Dresden on 16th April, just four days after Richard, Else, Rosi and Klaus had left. They had just missed being caught up in the bombing of Dresden twice!

Klaus was making good progress in his development. Rosi writes that "Klaus is starting to grip things with his hands and holds his head up by himself. He is starting to sit up and stretches his hands in the air." On 8 May 1945, Rosi writes in her diary: "PEACE!! The war is over! And the birds are singing." She announces proudly that "Klaus can drink from a cup and stand up by himself in his pram, very upright." They now have to protect him from falling out of the pram with a harness. "His first tooth has come through but he has a slight fever." Now the war is over and troops can stop fighting, Rosi is anxious to find her husband Günter. She needs him to be a father again, taking financial and parental responsiblity for their new-born son. However her father, Richard, thinks it is still too dangerous and won't let her go. Passage by boat on the Elbe to Hamburg continued to be impossible at this time but hoping this would change, they travelled south to Aussig (Usti nad Labem) on the 30 July and arrived the following day.

Aussig was an ethnically German town in the Sudetenland, northern Bohemia, on the Elbe about 80 km upstream from Dresden. At the end of the war, many local Germans were taken prisoner by the town's Czech administration. All Germans had to wear white armbands (just as the Nazis had forced Jews to wear yellow armbands). They were used as forced labour in the town. When the Koschels realized what was going on, they left at once. Just hours later, on the 31 July 1945, a big explosion occured. A group of Germans had been ordered to perform the dangerous task of gathering unused war weapons and munitions, including grenades and bazookas, and storing them for safety in a warehouse. That afternoon an explosion in the warehouse killed about 20 Germans and 7 Czechs. The rumour circulated that "Werewolf" Germans had caused the explosion as an act of sabotage. "Werewolves" were an SS fight-to-the-death movement. This rumour triggered a massacre of ethnic Germans in the town. They were beaten up and thrown into the Elbe from the bridge. As they tried to swim to shore, they were shot. Many people were lynched and their bodies also thrown into the river. It was a terrible and bloody massacre. An enquiry later concluded that the explosion had, in fact, been executed by a Czech communist, Bedrich Pockorny, with the object of putting blame on the Werewolves and thus triggering anti-German feelings. In that respect he was very successful.

The Koschel family, having missed the massacre by the skin of their teeth, were in Pirna on the 1st of August and saw the bodies from Aussig floating down the river. They watched a man on the quay pulling them out of the water using a long boat-hook. He told them that, so far, they had dragged a total of 1,800 corpses out of the river. This massacre was reported in a 49th anniversary remembrance article published in a German newspaper on Sunday 31 July 1994. Rosi kept this as a cutting and may have been the woman quoted in the article. Else was very traumatized by the event.

After this horror, the Koschels must have felt keen to move on. On the 2nd of August, they caught a train from Pirna to Glauchau and slept overnight in the train. Next day they continued on to Eisenach and then Dorndorf. Again they stayed overnight in the train in the woods by the border. They returned to Pirna where Richard bought sets of stamps (franked 10.8.1945) and then they moved on to Wuppertal for several days. At the beginning of September they went to Magdeburg, Badeleben, Leipzig and then back to Pirna. They obviously liked it there and settled in for a month. The diary contains lists of food items allocated to the family to live on: it seemed to be a peaceful domestic pause in their wanderings. On 11 October they returned to Magdeburg by lorry and stayed there until the 22 October. Finally they went on to Salzwedel, about 120 km south of Hamburg, to stay with the Altmann family. The Altmanns were long-standing family friends, treated as "Aunty and Uncle". They had a home in Wellingsbüttel, part of the prosperous green northern suburbs of Hamburg. After staying a month with them, the Koschels continued north and reached Hamburg on the 23 November 1945.

The Koschels had, by this time, spent almost a year on the move since they left Krakau. They cheated death several times. The moves to towns on the Elbe indicates (confirmed by Klaus) that they were hoping to return to Hamburg via a river boat. The bombing of Dresden foiled that plan. The diary does not explain why they went where they did. They may have gone to friends and other distant relatives but it is hard to think they were just having a long holiday in the circumstances. The Koschel's home was in one of the few apartment houses in Zimmerstraße that had not been burnt out. It had been saved from the incendiary bombs by their friends, the Maurer family. They had emerged from the cellar after the third RAF Gomorrah bombing raid and had torn down burning curtains in the apartments, thus preventing the fire from taking hold. They had a glazier's shop on one corner of the building at semi-basement level. Ane Marie Barth's fish shop had been on the adjacent corner (Chapter 1).

When Richard, Else, Rosi and Klaus finally returned to Hamburg, they moved back into their old apartment. About a year later their nephew, Werner Hamelmann, was released from his PoW camp (Chapter 15). Many of his mother's letters had not reached him while he was imprisoned, so he was uncertain about where his family were now living. His first thought was to go to Zimmerstraße, the street where all the families had been living before the 1943 bombing raids. Werner found that a few of the houses were still intact. He went to the apartment where the Koschels had been living and rang the doorbell. He was totally amazed when Klaus, who was nearly two years old, opened the door and gave him a cheeky cry of "Borsche! Borsche!" (a corruption of "Bursche Bursche" which translates roughly into "Watch out, I know you did it!", according to the adult Klaus.) Little Klaus was the first member of the family that Werner met after his two years in the PoW camps. The Koschels were very pleased to see Werner alive and well after the tribulations of the war years. After a coffee and a long talk about their war years, they directed him to Richardstraße 29a where his mother Trudel's new apartment was almost complete.

The Koschels were obliged to share their apartment with strangers because of the acute housing shortage. (They were lucky to have a home to go back to, at all.) However, they needed more room as Klaus got older. Richard applied for a new apartment and eventually got one on 1 Nov 1950, in Finkenau 30. This was, conveniently, a short walk from Trudel's new apartment so the two sisters could meet up regularly for a chat over coffee and cakes. Some time after they moved in, they acquired an additional member of the family, a monkey from Brazil, called "Miko". He was great fun to watch and play with. The Koschels settled in Finkenau for many peaceful years, until the end of their days.

Chapter Thirteen

Oldendorf on the Lüneburger Heide

(G)oldendorf: a little heaven near the gates of hell.

After we had been bombed out of our apartment in Hamburg in July 1943, my mother Dolly, sister Annemarie and I had spent a year in rural Bavaria as refugees (Chapter 9). As the war moved on, new refugees came from the east, from Vienna and other parts of Austria, putting pressure on us northern refugees. We needed to find a new home, again.

Our father, Maximilian, enquired with the authorities to find us a place nearer Hamburg that would take us in. South of Hamburg lies the Lüneburger Heide (Lüneburg Heath) which is mostly beautiful open heath and woodland with a few small towns and villages. Large parts of it are now designated as National Parks. Max managed to find us a place there on a farm in Oldendorf, a small village about 25 km north of Celle and 5 km south of Hermannsburg. In the autumn of 1944, we left Frontenhausen and went back to Hamburg, staying for only one night. We met up with our father, Max, who was looking much healthier than when we saw him last, on day release from the hospital. Trudel and Opa were still staying with the Völkers in Lustadt. We went to see our old home in Zimmerstraße 38. The house was just a hollow shell, everything gone, burnt out. Our mother stood in front of it shocked and saddened. She remembered the apartment with the family and the happy times we had had there. She recalled a beautiful antique musical box, originally belonging to Maximilan's parents. Along with all our other possessions, it was now just ashes.

The following day we got on a train which had no carriages, just open trucks. As there were no seats, we had to sit on our suitcase or the floor. The train set off, travelling sometimes very slowly. At one point a plane flew low over us: it seemed to be looking at the train which made us worry that it might attack, but it flew on. Eventually we arrived in Beckedorf, a small village on Lüneburg Heath. This was close to Bergen and the adjacent village of Belsen which were also quiet rural places in which nothing much happened, as far as we knew. Their significance was not revealed until much later.

My mother, sister and I climbed out of the truck, brushed ourselves down and looked around. It was a cloudy, mild afternoon in September 1944. The landscape was very flat and open, with fields, wild heath and woodlands all around. After our uncomfortable journey we were stiff and tired but we still had quite a long walk ahead of us. However, it was good to be somewhere new in such lovely surroundings. We walked to Oldendorf along a lane bordered by apple trees. Close to the outskirts of the village, by the side of the lane, I noticed a simple wooden cross with a military helmet on it. A name was written on the cross and there was a small bunch of faded flowers at the foot. We stopped and wondered why it was here in such an unlikely place. Our mother said that it couldn't be a grave, perhaps it was a memorial for the death of a local man.

Our mother encouraged us on. She carried a small brown suitcase with our few possessions and held my hand. In my other hand I was holding my beloved teddy bear close to me. I was three and a half years old. My sister, Annemarie was striding ahead. She was six years old, blonde and beautiful. I looked up to her and loved her, even though she was rather bossy to me sometimes. We were getting close to our destination, a farmhouse in Oldendorf, home of the Martens family who had agreed to take us in as refugees. This was to be our new home but we had no idea for how long. The war was still ongoing but after the D-day landings, many people thought it would soon be over.

At a road junction, a large traditional barn-shaped farmhouse faced us. It was typical of the local style, half-timbered with brick inlay and a large tiled roof. Dormer windows were let into two sides at first floor level. The front double-doors were made of oak, beautifully carved in the style of church altar panels. A plaque on the side of the house read "Erbaut (built) 1923, H & E Martens". My mother knocked on the door. We were greeted by Frau Martens and led into the large dark hall. There was an open staircase leading to the first floor. We went up and were shown into a couple of small rooms that were to be our home. The first room was a sitting room with bare polished pitch-pine floorboards. It had a small fireplace, a shabby sofa, a table with a couple of chairs and a small cupboard. Leading off it was the bedroom with two beds and a wash stand by the window. We were given some lunch in the Martens' dining room and while we sat there, the geese were cackling outside very noisily. Our mother felt at ease and said, "I think it's going to be very nice here."

Despite the terrible things going on in the war, life in the village was pretty idyllic; the war seemed far away. The Martens' farm consisted of the house and farmyard with beautiful large barns that had the traditional pair of horses' heads carved into the tops of the gable-end beams. The village was very picturesque with many large trees and wide open green spaces. It had several large barns, some very old, all with the horses' heads on the gables. Some had original thatch and some tile roofs. There was only one small shop in Oldendorf which sold flour, rice and other staples. The nearest shops with a wider range of goods were in Beckedorf and Hermannsburg and we had to walk to get there, although occasionally our mother got a lift with Herr Martens on his horse-drawn cart.

Oldendorf had a very small church which was also half-timbered. It had a square tapered wooden tower and a tiled roof. There was a First World War memorial in front of it. Herr Martens was a very kind and religious man. He played the trumpet, sometimes in the church during services, but it was just too loud there, really overpowering in such a confined space: I had to put my fingers in my ears. He was very good to us during our time in Oldendorf and Frau Martens was also a very kind and sympathetic woman. Their son had been sent off to the war. To their great sorrow, he was killed in battle and they never saw him again. (Perhaps the memorial cross we had seen by the side of the lane was dedicated to him: we never found out.) Fortunately for them, they also had three lovely daughters who were in their early 20s. They worked on the farm, feeding the pigs, looking after the chickens, milking the cows, making butter and cheese, picking apples, cooking dinners and very many other farm chores.

Downstairs, there was a family sitting room at the front of the farm house where the ancient art of spinning was still practised by the Martens girls, Emma, Erika and Elisabeth. It was fascinating to watch how they pulled a skein of wool while working the treddle to spin it into thread. Life in this village was very self-sufficient, it had

Peter and Anna, Oldendorf, 1945

not changed much over the centuries. There was a large kitchen at the back, overlooking the garden. It had a sink, a big solid-fuel stove, a few cupboards and a table in the middle. A door led from the right side of the kitchen, into a small barn which held pig sties. At the far end of this barn was a deep-pit latrine with two wooden seats next to each other over the pit, as in Roman days. Between the two seats there was a small board giving a modicum of privacy during the occasional double occupancy. A latrine straight off a pigsty, leading into a kitchen, is not a great idea. The smell was dreadful – but somehow, the pigs got used to it.

As a consequence of this arrangement, the kitchen was full of flies, the walls and ceiling were black with them. I thought all kitchens were like this: I was quite surprised when I saw a kitchen without black walls. The flies didn't seem to worry the Martens family: all the food was prepared and cooked there. I often used to stand next to Frau Martens when she was chopping up Speck (a type of bacon). She usually gave me the odd titbit as I watched her hopefully.

There was no bathroom in the house so our mother had to buy a tin bath. Bath days were usually once a week. Our mother would heat buckets of water on the stove in the scullery and carry them upstairs. Anna and I were bathed first in our little sitting room. Then Dolly would top it up with another bucketful of hot water and bathe herself. All the water had to be carried up and down the stairs every bath day.

Despite being on a farm, food was in pretty short supply. This was because most of the produce of the farm was commandeered by the Nazi Government for the war effort. There were severe punishments if the food handed over fell short of the expected yields. Apart from the pigs and chickens, the farm had cows for milk and some fields for potatoes and other crops, including sugar beet. Next to the kitchen, before entering the pig-sty, there was the scullery which held another solid-fuel stove. The Martens girls chopped up the sugar beets and boiled them in a big cauldron on this stove. The broth was tested by putting a spoonful onto a saucer. When crystals of sugar formed, the broth was left to cool and crystalize out.

To help with the work, there were forced-labour Poles living on the farm. They did not live in the farmhouse at all. Their life was very mediaeval: they had simple straw beds in little alcoves in one of the barns. They also had a small area of the barn separated off where they could gather and eat together. They washed at the pump in the farmyard. Dolly sometimes gave them some extra potatoes or other food when it was available. They showed their appreciation on one occasion by making an aeroplane out of pieces of wood and gave it to me. It didn't fly very well but it was a very exciting toy to have: I gave my teddy rides on it.

Our mother also helped with the work on the farm and was given a few eggs, a piece of cheese or some German sausage now and again. Nothing was ever wasted. If milk went sour our mother would pour it into a fine muslin cloth, tie the corners together and hang it up over a bowl to drip. Over night it formed into a portion of cottage cheese in the cloth. We ate it with bread or sometimes it was used in cooking. It was usually delicious but occasionally it went bitter. Stale bread was turned into a bread pudding in the oven. There were apple trees in the garden and also along the lane: we were allowed to eat these freely.

Apart from the Poles, boys and girls living in the village also helped with the farm work. They joined in at hay-making time when everybody was needed. The older boys were put to work sometimes using poles to keep the cows from straying into the river. We younger children were also press-ganged into the job of removing potato-blight beetles from the leaves of the potato plants in the fields. This was labour-intensive work that required sharp eyes and little fingers but it was an interesting challenge, for a while at least. We were rewarded with some sweet treat at the end.

Not long after we had settled in Oldendorf, winter arrived, bringing thick snow for many weeks. There were several children in the village. We had great fun running around, playing snowballs and building snow-men together. Someone brought a sledge along. The landscape was very flat so there were few down-hill runs, apart from the short slope down to the river, which was obviously too dangerous. So we took it in turns to pull and be pulled around the village on the sledge by one of the older children.

St Nicholas's Day was on the 6th of December when the *real* Santa Klaus, Saint Nicholas, who was sometimes dressed as a bishop, brought small presents to good children. His side-kick, Knecht Ruprecht or Schwarze Peter (Black Peter) did unspeakably nasty things to naughty children or even took them away in his sack! The kind, present-giving Saint, traditionally dressed in green, has been merged into Father Christmas in most countries and now wears red, popularized by a Coca Cola advertising campaign which started in 1933 in the USA. However, in Germany at that time, the original tradition was still alive. Annemarie and I both put a shoe (we didn't have any clogs) out on the bedroom window-sill before going to bed on the night of the 5th of December. We must have both been good children because in the morning, with the sun sparkling on the frost and snow, there were some exciting goodies in our shoes. We had some nuts, ginger bread and sweets wrapped in pretty paper: not a lot by present day standards, but for us, an exciting treat.

We still had Christmas Day to look forward to when we were visited by Father Christmas! The tradition for present-giving in Germany was to have a side table separated into areas with the presents for each person neatly arranged on it. We weren't allowed into the sitting room until all this had been prepared. It was a very tense and exciting moment. There was a lot of loud knocking at the front door, which was rather frightening, until Herr Martens, dressed as Santa Claus, came in at last. Because of all his white whiskers, we didn't know it was Herr Martens. We were all given presents. Finally, Annemarie and I had to do our little performance piece. This was the famous poem about a doll taken to see Doctor Pillermann because it is sick. In the first verse, the doll hasn't eaten for three days, it sits silently, is not even tempted by sweetmeats and hangs its arms as if dead:-

"Lieber Doktor Pillermann,
guck dir bloss mein Püppchen an,
Drei Tage hat es nichts gegessen
hat immer so stumm da gesessen,
es will nicht einmal Zuckerbrot
die Arme hängen ihr wie tot."

Annemarie had a doll she had been given in Hamburg that she was very fond of. Our mother made it a new outfit every Christmas. Annemarie enjoyed dressing the doll, combing her hair and making her look very smart: the antithesis of the Püppchen in the verse.

The snow lasted for many weeks, including on the roads which were not cleared. The landscape was very beautiful, especially when the setting sun turned red as we watched it from our window at bed-time in the farmhouse. Herr Martens had a large horse-drawn sleigh which he used in winter to go to nearby villages to fetch and carry food and other farm produce. We occasionally got a ride in it which was great fun. He told us he had borrowed it from Santa Claus after his recent visit. We weren't sure but we didn't *really* believe him.

Easter was also a jolly time. A profusion of daffodils came out and there was blossom on the fruit trees. I remember we had a traditional egg hunt in the garden. My sister and I ran around looking for eggs. To my consternation, Annemarie quickly found a couple but I still hadn't found one. I went on looking but to no avail. Then my mother surreptitiously indicated with her eyes and a nod of her head towards a bush nearby and there, I saw an egg. Hooray! They were all hard boiled chicken's eggs, painted in bright colours. They should have been so easy to find! Of course there was no possibility of chocolate in those days but an extra egg was a wonderful treat. The Martens had hens running around in the back garden. They were kept not only for eggs but also to eat, but this was a rare luxury. Frau Martens had a wooden block on which she laid the bird's neck. One quick whack with a small axe (mind your fingers) and the head was off. Sometimes the hen ran around for a while without its head. We thought this was black magic: very disturbing.

One of the major events in the farming season was the killing of a pig. The regulations at that time permitted the slaughter of only one pig per year. This was not just red tape, it was strictly enforced by the Nazi regime. In September 1940 a farmer in Rostock was beheaded for killing a pig without permission: a terrible and primitive punishment.

The day arrived when the authorized slaughterer was due to come. My sister and I were told that, the following day, there would be a "Schweinschlacht" and that our help would be needed. Next morning we were woken just before dawn. We got dressed and had our usual breakfast of a piece of rye bread and a cup of milk. The sun was just showing above the horizon when we all gathered in the farmyard. This was a big event, everybody on the farm had to be there, including Annemarie and me, although we were only young children. There was an indefinable tension in the air, which is why, I think, I remember it well. A large pig was led to a wooden block in the middle of the farmyard. It seemed unaware of any danger. Members of the family and the farm workers surrounded it. The pig started to get a bit restless. Everyone closed in to hold it in position at the block. Annemarie and I had been told that we must help by holding the pig's tail, which we did. This was obviously not a practical necessity but a token of complicity in a sacrificial act. I wonder if this "ceremony" had its origins in the distant past.

The pig got more nervous and everyone held it down more

firmly. The slaughterer then hit the pig hard on the head with a stout wooden club, which stunned it. It slumped onto the block. He then cut the pigs throat with one smooth stroke of a large sharp knife. Blood flowed freely from its neck into the bucket which had been placed ready by the block. Blood went on flowing for quite a while. The pig was still and slumped further. Eventually the body was carried away to a barn and hung up by its back legs, which were tied together, over a bucket to catch the remaining blood. Annemarie and I were horrified by the whole thing. We were allowed to go back to our room. Our mother told us later how she was given the task of making the Blutwurst (black pudding). The bucket of blood was put on the stove in the scullery over a low flame. As the blood warmed up, Dolly stirred it with her arm for over an hour until the blood thickened and set. Chopped-up Speck was often mixed into it.

Up the road near to the farm was a similar house where another family, the Bartels, lived. Who we got to know very well. They also had three daughters. Emma Martens married Otto, a local man and continued to live in the village. She wrote and published poetry written in the local ancient dialect, Plattdeutsch, which was spread all over the north-western plain of Europe including Hamburg. It was still in use when I went back there in the mid 1950s. My friend Gerd's grandmother spoke only Plattdeutsch and Gerd had to translate it for me, although it is actually closer to English than Hochdeutsch (the accepted present-day pan-germanic language of Martin Luther). Dutch is an extant branch of Plattdeutsch. The second sister, Erika, was carried off to England by a conquering British soldier, "Curly", (see below).

When Annemarie reached the age of seven (August 1945) she was sent to school in the village. Each pupil had the use of a Schreibtafel mit Kreide (a slate and a piece of chalk). Most lessons involved using this to write words or do arithmatic. So they learnt their letters and numbers. Unfortunately, "Sieg heil!"

and the Nazi salute were also a manditory part of the curriculum then (but fortunately it didn't stick). The school day started at 7 or 8 o'clock and finished at noon or 1 pm when all the pupils went home for their Mittagessen. That was when we ate our main cooked meal together in our room upstairs.

After lunch, in fine weather, Annemarie would take off her shoes and run around outside to play with her friends. We felt so free. There were no cars to worry about, just the occasional horse and cart. The roads were cobbled and there were no pavements, just grass and plenty of open space. Annemarie had a particular friend called Liselotte. They were always playing together in the village. Annemarie loved the freedom of the place and felt constrained when some years later we were living in a town and she had to wear shoes outside. The open country of the Heide stretched out for miles in all directions and we often went there for walks. In the summer we picked blueberries, cranberries and wild strawberries, which were tiny but delicious. In the autumn there were blackberries and wild mushrooms of various types. Occasionally we would find the bright yellow-orange "Pfifferlinge" and the more common "Steinpilze" (stone mushrooms). The average German, unlike the average Englishman, knew which types of fungi were edible and which you should avoid. The wild countryside was so beautiful and full of interesting plants and animals. Snakes were quite common: we often saw them slithering around in the grass or undergrowth. We children were cautious but not really afraid of them.

Running through Oldendorf is a lovely sparkling river, the Ötze, about 10-12 metres wide, with clean, quite fast running, water. It had a small bridge (now gone) over it, just a short walk down from the farm. Near the bridge there were grassy banks which was a popular place for the villagers to gather. On long hot summer days people would meet there and go swimming in the river. Annemarie and I couldn't swim but we loved splashing about in the water by the bank. Sometimes there were swimming races, back and forth across the river, which we enjoyed watching. Our mother and other neighbours brought picnics which we ate sitting on the grass, while people rowed past in small boats, creating sometimes a happy carnival atmosphere.

One day I was with my mother, walking back from a nearby village. We were approaching the Ötze bridge when we heard a droning sound above us getting louder. It was a small plane coming towards us. We had no time to look for markings. My mother quickly and firmly pulled me down the bank and under the bridge where we hid. She was very nervous. We waited there until the sound of the plane had died away. We didn't know which side of the war it was on but my mother had instinctively run for cover. Her experience in Hamburg during the war made her, very sensibly, wary of all aircraft. Later we discovered that, some time after D-day, an RAF squadron had been stationed in Wunstorf which was not far from Oldendorf. The plane may well have been one of the RAF Hawker Typhoons which were stationed there.

When we first got to Oldendorf (Autumn 1944) our father, Maximilian was still stationed in the Horst Wessel Barracks in Hamburg. When he got leave, he would make short visits to us in Oldendorf. Sometimes he took us for walks in the Heide: Annemarie remembers sitting in a meadow on a sunny afternoon while Max made a daisy-chain and put it on her head. He got on well with the Martens and made himself useful around the farm, although he admitted to our mother that occasionally, he pinched an egg, pricked and sucked it there and then in the hen coop. At bedtime, Annemarie and I would go to bed as usual in our bedroom. Later, when it was their bedtime, our father would squeeze in with me and our mother with Annemarie. It was a bit of a squash but we all slept well.

Annemarie was a beautiful girl with long blonde hair, usually in plaits. I had been fitted with glasses by this time to compensate for my squint, which was still the same as when it first happened, during the bombing of Hamburg. From letters of Max to Dolly

(Chapter 15), he shows that he clearly loved us all. However, perhaps because I was a boy and wore glasses, he seemed to be a little more stern with me. Annemarie was clearly his favourite. I had a set of wooden blocks, with the letters of the alphabet on them, which I used to play with on the window-sill, looking out across the fields and heathland. My mother taught me the sounds of the letters and apparently I was fairly quick learning how to spell out simple words including my own name. I was also given paper and coloured pencils for drawing and writing which kept me amused. Perhaps because of the glasses and the writing, I was nicknamed the "professor" although I had no idea what a professor was.

Arrival of the Allies

After the D-Day landings in June 1944, Allied forces had been pushing their way north through France, the Netherlands and into Germany. Churchill, with great foresight, urged that the Allies should advance rapidly to reach the Baltic coast before the Russians got there, to prevent them from occupying German territory too far to the west. In late spring 1945, two British soldiers entered Oldendorf on motor bikes. They were fore-runners of the forces making their way north to Hamburg. My mother spotted them from upstairs. Just to be on the safe side, she waved a white pillow case of surrender out of the window. Very excited but also nervous, she went downstairs and ventured out to see them. Suddenly she thought, "Oh, I'd better put my hands up" and did so. The soldiers were surprised when she spoke to them in English. She told them she was British and said, "Are any of you here from London? Have you got a British newspaper?" She hadn't seen one for years. Dolly continued the conversation with them but found that, as she had been speaking only German for many years, occasionally the odd German word would involuntarily jump into her speech. This caused concern for a while until she convinced them that she was genuinely British.

Some days later we watched from the window as a group of British tanks came trundling over the heath and fields in our direction. They encountered no resistance. As they entered the village, the tank tracks broke many of the cobblestones in the road. A small company of British soldiers looked for places to billet themselves. They found the Big House which belonged to a rich family in Oldendorf. It may have been the village manor house in earlier days. The occupants were firmly told to leave and most of the officers and men occupied it. In late July when school finished and was closed, the soldiers used it as a holding camp for the Polish forced labour workers. They were held there until they could be repatriated to their home country.

Our mother went to the Big House and offered to act as an interpreter for the soldiers, which was readily accepted. Payment came in the form of food: chocolate, fruit such as oranges (which we had never seen before) sausages and tinned foods. One day, when she was at the Big House, a soldier was complaining that one of the loaves they were making in the kitchen had been burnt in the oven and he would have to throw it away. "Ooh, can I have it please" our mother said. She brought it home, cut off the burnt bits and we ate it with home-made jam. What a treat! Learning from this, Annemarie and her friend Liselotte picked a bunch of wild flowers on the heath. They knocked on the kitchen door of the Big House and very sweetly, curtsied and handed the posy to the cook. He took it, thanked them, went inside and came back with a big handful of sultanas for them to eat. Clever girls!

Dolly was asked if she would be willing to wash clothes for the soldiers. She was happy to do so. While she was ironing a shirt one day, she found it had a button missing. She looked through her button collection but the only one she had of the same size and colour had a swastika on it. She wondered whether to sew it on (as a joke) but decided against it, using a plain button instead. When the corporal came to collect the laundry, she told him about the swastika button to give him a laugh. He said, "Thank God you didn't use it – that shirt belongs to the Captain. He could have had you shot!"

The British company stayed a few months in the village. To keep the troops from getting bored and maintain their morale, the officers organized Saturday night dances. They used one of the big barns in the village which provided the perfect setting for a jolly evening. A scratch band of soldiers was assembled to play the music. It sometimes included Herr Martens who offered to play his trumpet. He was brilliant! Here was a setting where he could really let rip, unlike the church, where it was utterly deafening. A plentiful supply of good German beer was made available. All the local girls were invited of course. This was a rare chance in a normally quiet village, for them to meet the British soldiers and have some fun. There were no young German men in the village, all able-bodied fellows had been called up into the forces but some of the Poles came along. Friendships with the local girls naturally followed. A young soldier, nicknamed Curly, got to know Erika Martens. They met several times at the dances and their friendship blossomed into love. He proposed marriage and she accepted. Erika and Curly got married in England after the war when he was demobbed. They settled down happily in his home town of Stoke-on-Trent.

One day a small British tank turned up at the farm. One of the soldiers asked my mother if she would be willing to come with them to act

Erika Martens, 1945.

as an interpreter. Annemarie was playing with her friends but my mother didn't want to leave me unsupervised, so she asked whether she could take me with her. It looked like an exciting trip for a small boy. Off we went. It was dark and cramped inside the tank with just one small window to look out of. There was a group of Polish workers living outside the village, in a house located a little way into the woods. They had kicked out the original inhabitants and taken it over. The Poles were in the middle of lunch when we got there, and were caught unawares. With my mother translating, the soldiers told the Poles that they had half an hour to pack up their belongings. Then a lorry would come to take them to a camp where they would stay for a while until they could be sent back to their native Poland to be free men again! However, when the soldiers weren't looking, some of the Poles jumped out of the back window and disappeared into the woods. Even though they were used as forced labour in Germany, they knew by then that the Russians had occupied Poland. They feared the Russians so much that they preferred to stay and take their chances in Germany under Allied occupation. At the end of the visit, the Tommys took us back to Oldendorf in the tank. It was an unusual and exciting adventure for a four-year old!

Some time later, a company of American troops took over from the British troops and billeted themselves in the village. They were more brash and criminal. They ordered everyone in the village to hand over their radios, watches and cameras which they kept as "spoils of war". Herr Martens was very upset because they took his gold watch which was a valuable family heirloom. He asked my mother whether she could try to get it back for him. So Dolly went to the Big House, explained the situation and asked very nicely (as an attractive and intelligent young woman) if Herr Martens could possibly have his watch back. Surprisingly, they returned it and he was absolutely delighted!

A short time after the surrender of Germany in May 1945,

parcels from England were permitted. We started to get them in Oldendorf from Uncle Eric, our mother's brother. He had been a fire warden in London throughout the war. During the bombing in Hamburg, my Aunt Trudel would point up to any RAF plane in the sky and say, "That's your Uncle Eric up there!" It was obviously a joke but the Second World War was a civil war to our family. Eric was a very kind, thoughtful and caring man so when parcels were permitted, he started sending us things that were hard to get in Germany. This included food such as cheese, ham and sugar. One day a parcel arrived containing tea and soap. It had been damaged in transit so that some of the soap had been broken up and got mixed with the tea. These things were too precious to be thrown away so our mother spent a long time separating them. Tea tasting of soap was horrible, but soap with a subtle aroma of tea was actually very pleasant. It could catch on.

We were still living in Oldendorf in December 1945 for our second Christmas. This time our father Maximilian and his sister Trudel came to celebrate it with us. We had a lovely Christmas: it was so exciting all being together again after such a long time. My mother later wrote to Werner who was still languishing in a PoW camp somewhere:

(11. 3. 1946): We want to see you again very much and I hope it won't be much longer. Life must be very difficult and sad for you. We do our best to comfort your mother. But you will come home again, that is your mother's only hope and for that she is running round finding things for your new home. Trudel has visited us here in Oldendorf and found it very nice: the Martens family love having her. They are very kind people and the children have a good life here. I was so happy to have left Bavaria. I have received a letter from my relatives in London, it was lovely to hear from them again. Peter and Annemarie

are growing up fast. Annemarie goes to school and Peter paints and plays: they are lovely kids.

Your mother and Max spent Christmas here, it was our best Christmas since we had to leave Hamburg. Tante Trudel must have tapped Father Christmas very firmly on the shoulder: they brought a load of presents with them. How does she do it? She is going to fetch Opa back to Hamburg (from Lustadt), he is feeling very home-sick. Dear Werner, I hope that things aren't too bad for you and you aren't suffering from hunger. Is there anything we can do for you somehow? I hope the time passes quickly until you come home again.

Chapter Fourteen

The Sinking of the Cap Arcona, May 1945

The Neuengamme Concentration Camp prisoners were marched out of one hell only to be bombed to death in another.

Before the second world war, my uncle, Adam Hamelmann, worked as Chief Steward on the Cap Arcona, a luxury

The cruise ship Cap Arcona in Rio, Brazil, 1936.

liner which was the pride of the Hamburg Süd Line. She was named after the northern-most point (Kap Arkona), a beauty spot on the island of Rügen in the Baltic Sea. Built by Blohm und Voss in their Hamburg shipyards, she was launched in 1927. The ship was 206 m long, had three funnels and a full-size tennis court on deck. She was the fastest ship on the route between Hamburg and Buenos Aires and other ports in South America, carrying passengers in both luxurious first class accommodation and as steerage-class emigrants. In the 1930's many Germans travelled to South America for tourism, trade and settlement. The facilities and service were among the best in those glory days of cruise liners and it was Adam's job to ensure that the highest standards were maintained. During his time on the ship, he regularly wrote letters to his wife Trudel (my aunt) and his two sons, Werner and Walter. It is from these letters and the recollections of Werner (some recorded on tape) that the unique aspects of this story can be told.

In 1940, shortly after the start of the second world war, the Cap Arcona was requisitioned by the German Navy (Kriegsmarine). It was taken into the Baltic Sea and docked in the harbour of Gdynia (a Polish harbour town, renamed by the Germans as Gotenhafen) which is in a sheltered bay close to the Hanseatic city of Danzig (Gdansk). There it became a floating luxury hotel for officers of the Wehrmacht throughout the war. Adam, as a civilian, continued to fulfill his role as Chief Steward. As an unforeseen irony, the Cap Arcona was used to portray the RMS Titanic in the 1943 Nazi propaganda film about the sinking of that ship. The film plot shows greedy, rich capitalists in London cutting costs on lifeboats and safety equipment and pushing the speed of the Titanic beyond its statutory safety limits, in order to win the fastest Atlantic crossing record and thus make a lot of money on bets.

On the 9th of October 1943 at 1 pm there was an Allied

aircraft bombing raid on Gotenhafen: both the town and harbour were attacked. Adam wrote to Trudel:

> (12.10.1943): There were over a hundred dead and injured. Thirteen ships were destroyed but miraculously, our Cap Arcona was left undamaged. Nine heavy bombs fell left and right of her but she was not directly hit. The hospital ship Stuttgart was very heavily bombed. 40 people were killed and it was completely burnt out. It was then towed out and sunk in deeper water. 62 of the Anglo-Americans were shot down. The fear is that they will return soon. There is no bunker and it is very dangerous to remain on the ship.

Adam prepared for the possibility of future air raids by packing a small suitcase with a few clothes and necessary items, including his winter coat, and took them onshore to the nearby town of Adlershorst (Orłowo). He also wrote to Trudel (who was at that time in the Pfalz with Adam's aunt and uncle) that he has sent her four packages of goodies including cigarettes, a bottle of vermouth and four tins of rabbit. He warns her, "The rabbit may be partly cooked because the tins were near the fire in the kitchens when the aircraft warning alarms went off." He suggests that Trudel could share the cigarettes with her hosts, the Krügers, as well as with her brother Maximilian, my father, who returned from Russia half-starved and severely wounded and was now in a hospital in Rothenburg, Hannover (Ch 9). It seems bizarre nowadays to think that hospital patients should be sent cigarettes.

Adam was always optimistic about the outcome of the war. He writes:

> (5.11.1943): I think the war cannot last much longer and then we can all be together again. I have managed to obtain, without ration coupons, sets of china and cutlery

and bought a packing case so that we can slowly gather household goods together again for our new home after the war. Please do not worry so much about the future. We will win the war, without a doubt. You must make this your strong belief too and then you will see, your worries will dwindle and you will be happy and healthy again. We still have each other and our two boys. Although we lost everything in the bombing of Hamburg, we can rebuild our home and be lucky and happy again.

Adam, on board ship, had very little to spend his salary on which, as Chief Steward, was substantial. He therefore bought up things that would be needed to furnish their new home after the war and other items that came his way. He had already bought Trudel a fox-fur coat as a Christmas present. He also purchased an electric room heater, some cutlery and a few other items which he sent to Hamburg in anticipation of Christmas. Unfortunately, after all that preparation, he couldn't get time off to enjoy the festivities with his family (and find out if the tins of rabbit *were* nicely cooked). In the New Year he managed to buy a goose which he sent to Hamburg for Walter's 17th birthday and included some cigarettes for Werner. He was very pleased when Trudel came to stay with him on the ship for a couple of weeks a short time later.

During 1944, the Bay of Gdynia proved to be free of any major air attacks and life onboard the ship continued smoothly. In a letter to his family (1.3.1944) Adam writes that he has sent butter, bacon, lard and cigarettes to them. He urges Werner to try to get some leave to visit him on the ship. "Don't come in your civvies, I have a suit for you here. It's best if you come with an empty suitcase. Send me a telegram and I'll pick you up." Unfortunately, Werner's leave was suddenly cancelled and he was transferred to Camp Fallingbostel on Lüneburg Heath for a radio communication training course and then on to Norway (Chapter 10). Adam was very relieved that Werner was being sent to Norway, it is so much quieter than the Russian front. He writes to Trudel:

(20.3.1944): The decisive battle will come this year and I believe a good outcome will definitely be for our side. It doesn't look good for the enemy. Now it will depend on who has the strongest nerve; this time it will be the Germans.

Adam wrote again on the occasion of their forthcoming wedding anniversary which falls on the 12th of May:

(7.5.1944): It will be 21 years of happy marriage since the day I stood before God and the Law and said my "I do". Do you remember that my love? The years have gone by so fast. We were always happy and the times by your side with our children were so wonderful. Now, during this time of separation and deprivation, we must not lose our courage and hope; we must wait patiently for the time when we will be back in our own cosy home again. We must keep our nerve, believe in a just cause and stay healthy. There is absolutely no doubt that we will win this war!

Towards the end of 1944 (17.11.1944) Adam wrote to Trudel that they had heard nothing from their son Werner for a long time. Some time before, he had written to the Central Office of the Red Cross in Berlin giving his number (10456) and asking if they had news of him, one way or another. He had received no news. He also wrote to the German Red Cross. No news so far but that might mean that he is in a PoW camp. Knowing that his unit had gone to Normandy, Adam is optimistic that this is likely and Werner would be safe. Adam always expressed his optimism to Trudel but we don't know his true feelings.

By the middle of December 1944, there was still no news

about Werner. Adam repeats his theme that he was convinced that Germany will win the war. He was still trying to keep Trudel's spirits up (12.12.1944). He thinks the "strong west wall" cannot be overrun. "New weapons have been developed. Our enemies are worn out." His motto seems to be, "Krieg bis zum Sieg" (War until Victory). Is he still under the perpetual influence of the German propaganda machine, or is he just repeating the mantra to keep his own spirits up?

They start to make their Christmas plans. Adam hasn't got much to bring with him, supplies are meagre, but he has managed to get a goose. "What can you expect after six years of war?" He is looking forward to his eight day holiday with family and friends in Hamburg. He plans to arrive by train via Stettin and Lübeck on the 19th December early afternoon and hopes that Walter could meet him at the station. Trudel and Walter were living at this time with the Krüger family (Else and Bruno) in their large house in the Hoheneichen suburb of Hamburg. Apparently Walter gets on very well with their daughter Lucie. Opa Max will be joining them for Christmas. They had a happy reunion for a few days but there was a shadow over the jolities: there was still no news about Werner.

Adam's return journey to the Cap Arcona was horrendous. He wrote to Trudel:

(5.1.1945): I had a comfortable seat and the train was heated. It was fine until we got to Stettin. The journey from there to Gotenhafen was dreadful. The train was over-filled. I was in a part of the carriage with no heating and without windows, only venetian blinds through which a gale was blowing. I had to stand for eight hours and got back half frozen. I developed a nasty cold and packed myself off to bed. Yesterday I had to do the December accounts for the company. I am hoping to hear good news about Werner soon.

Adam sent congratulations to his younger son Walter (9.1.1945) on his 18th birthday and wished him all the best now that he has had his military call up. "I wish you lots and lots of 'soldier's luck'. I am sorry that I cannot be there to celebrate your birthday. I have had wonderful news, a card from Werner, writing that he is safe and sound in a British PoW camp." He thanks Fate for this. The long months of doubt as to whether he was alive or dead were dreadful for all of them. He hopes that Walter will have as much luck as his brother. Trudel has told him that Walter doesn't always wear his winter coat in the cold weather. Adam takes him to task. "This is very wrong of you. It is all too easy to catch a lung infection. It is the duty of every German man to defend his country and his loved ones." As in every year, he is firmly convinced that *this* year will bring the end of the war. This is the first time he has been right but not in the way he anticipated. This list of fatherly love and advice was the last letter Walter received from him.

The good news about Werner being alive was followed by bad news. In January 1945, Russian armies started to move west. People from East Prussia fled from the advancing troops. Adam wrote to Trudel:

(25.1.1945): Women and children from Danzig, Zoppott and Gotenhafen are being evacuated. The stations are packed with huge numbers of refugees waiting for trains to the west. Other ships, the Wilhelm Gustloff, the Hanse and the Antonia Delfino are full of refugees and ready to sail. It is time to keep cool and not despair. The Cap Arcona is steamed up, waiting for the order to go. (Russian forces had reached Elbing (Elblag) Poland only 70 km away.) We finally sailed with about 12,000 refugees, mostly women and children including 450 babies, but also many old people and wounded soldiers. We reached Neustadt (in the Bay of Lübeck) on 9 February after a seven day journey with four days stationary in fog. We had provisions for only 2-3 days for that many people. The refugees were given one bowl of soup per day but there was only enough bread for about a third of them. Many of the refugees have been saved with nothing but what they stood up in. Seven people died during the journey." (Considering the conditions and the state of the refugees, this was a mercifully low number.)

Two days earlier the Gustloff had sailed with 6,000 to 7,000 refugees. The ship was torpedoed by a Russian submarine. Most of the refugees were drowned, only 1100 people were rescued. The news about the Gustloff catastrophe soon spread around the Cap Arcona. Adam counted himself very lucky that they had arrived safely in the west. His ship was due to return to Gotenhafen to rescue more refugees. However, they couldn't because by then, the ship's engines needed repair. At first he thought "Thank God". But when he considered the masses of refugees and their misery, he realized it was his duty to go back east and rescue more people. The refugees on board packed the deck wherever they could find a place, while waiting to be taken off. It was a sorrowful sight of people in fear and desperation. When the ship first arrived at Neustadt, the crew did the best they could. Food was brought on board and the children got milk for the first time. But the refugees needed to find places to live on shore. It was difficult to know what to do with them. All means of transport had been disrupted by the bombing. Major railway lines had been cut, road and boat transport were badly affected. But at least the refugees were, for the time-being, safe from the Russian forces.

Adam sent another letter to Trudel from the Cap Arcona while it was anchored off Neustadt, Three days earlier he had come back from a couple of days leave to see her and their son Walter, which was all too short a time for him:

(19.2.1945): We cannot sail back to Gotenhafen because work on the engines is still not finished. We are waiting for a spare part and for the promised specialist engineer to complete the repair. We do not really want to go back east to Gotenhaven. It is better here, anchored off Neustadt, much safer than another sea journey past the Russian submarines and minefields in the Baltic. I have just heard from Captain Geertz that our ship is expected to be seaworthy on 23 February.

In Jacobs & Pool's book (*The Hundred Years Secret: Britain's Hidden World War II Massacre*, 2004) they write that on 20 February 1945, Captain Geertz shot himself in his cabin while berthed in Copenhagen, rather than face another voyage to Gotenhafen. But at that date, according to Adam's letter, he was on the Cap Arcona anchored off Neustadt, waiting for an engineer. However, it seems probable that he did commit suicide soon after that date because, on 27 Feb 1945, Captain Heinrich Bertram reported to the Hamburg Süd Line company that he had taken over command of the Cap Arcona. Unfortunately, Adam makes no mention of the fate of his colleague, Captain Geertz, in his letter. He probably did not want to upset Trudel with sad news. Adam continues in his letter to Trudel:

(19.2.1945): If you write quickly I will get your letter before we leave habour. Cross your fingers that we will meet again soon, safe and sound. But don't worry too much: a ship doesn't have to be sunk every time we do this trip. We haven't lost the war yet and our weapons haven't spoken their last word. But we will have lost the war when everyone believes we have.

He also sent Trudel a parcel containing butter and bacon which she had to collect from Hamburg central station the following morning. He urges her to give some to Walter as he is always hungry. He hopes to send her writing paper and soap-powder in the next parcel and signs off with a warm flow of love and affection, as always, with greetings also to his family and friends.

The Cap Arcona returned to Gotenhafen twice more and rescued wounded soldiers and refugees from the east but on these trips, they took them to Copenhagen. Soon after that, Adam wrote to Trudel (26.3.1945) that the ship is seaworthy and they will be heading directly back east to Gotenhafen soon. He must get his letter to the launch for posting. The final trip was on 30 March 1945. In a letter to Trudel (3.4.1945) he writes that he had heard that the recent attack on Hamburg was very intense but he hopes they got through it all right. He asks about how she is and all the family and friends and whether Werner has written from his PoW camp. Adam is not allowed to tell Trudel where he is so she cannot write back to him. However, he tells her they are not in Neustadt. Shortly after, in a letter from Copenhagen he writes:

(9.4.1945): I am sending this letter via a friend who is going to Germany. Our last trip from Gotenhafen went well. We brought circa 6,000 badly wounded soldiers and 2,000 refugees to safety with us. They will be cared for in Denmark. It is uncertain that the Cap Arcona can go back to Gotenhafen but, if needed, we are ready. Please do not to worry about me, all will be well. I send my greetings to all our family and friends.

Mechanical trouble with the Cap Arcona's turbines meant that she could not, in fact, undertake another long trip. She was therefore decommisioned by the German Navy and returned to Hamburg Süd's responsibility. She made the cruise from Copenhagen to Lübeck Bay very slowly and anchored off the coast near Neustadt again. In Adam's letter to Trudel (24.4.1945) he thanks her for her latest letter (brought by a friend) and for a parcel containing three bottles of wine. He is amazed that they arrived safely, or at all, considering the state of the country and the damage to the railway infrastructure. Trains from Hamburg could not get through directly any more. He and two friends on board drank one glass, and only one glass, of wine each. They drank a toast to the departure from the ship of one of the friends and to the health of Trudel and their two sons.

Their younger son, Walter, was due to be posted to the army camp in Oldenburg in Holstein which is about 25 km from Neustadt. Adam planned to see him every Sunday, by train if they are running, or by bicycle if not. He asked Trudel to tell Walter to write to him as soon as he gets there so that they may meet up. He will make sure that Walter gets some decent food on the ship. He thought it was possible they will get billetted again but he hopes to remain there by Neustadt. He has made plans to pack some of the items he has been buying for their future life together after the war in a packing-case and store it in the town so that Trudel can collect it later. By a lucky piece of foresight or instinct, he had it delivered to Trudel in Hamburg instead.

Two other ships, the SS Deutschland and the Thielbeck, along with the motor launch, Athen, were also brought to the Bay of Lübeck, apparently as part of the Nazi plans to deal with concentration camp prisoners. And thus began the third and final chapter in the history of this fine ship, the Cap Arcona. Firstly, it had been a luxury transatlantic liner in the 1930s. Secondly, it became a rescue ship evacuating wounded soldiers and refugees from East Prussia in early 1945. Finally, it was about to become a floating prison for concentration camp victims.

What happened next still leaves questions unanswered. It is thought that, with the war going badly for the Nazis, they wanted to complete an unexpected part of the "final solution" plan. During the course of many weeks, the SS had taken the Scandinavian concentration camp prisoners from all over the Reich and gathered them together in the Neuengamme concentration camp near Hamburg. This project was done under the "White Bus" scheme, organized by Count Folke Bernadotte, co-chairman of the Swedish Red Cross. Prisoners were driven in buses painted white with a red cross on the roof to indicate their purpose to the Allied Forces. In secret meetings with Himmler, Bernadotte agreed that these mostly Scandinavian "fellow Aryans" would be released in neutral Sweden or transported to the island of Fehmarn or to Mysen in Norway.

In the last two weeks of April 1945, with the Allies rapidly advancing north towards Hamburg, the Neuengamme camp was emptied. Over 9,000 prisoners were marched north to the Bay of Lübeck. They included Jewish and many other groups of forced labour prisoners as well as the White Bus Scandinavians. The SS command presumably wanted to conceal them from the advancing Allied troops. They could not afford any delay so those who fell on the way and couldn't go on, were ruthlessly shot and left where they lay. They literally formed a trail of bodies that was followed by British troops a few days later. At the Bay, the prisoners were transported onto the three ships by the motor launch Athen. They were locked in the holds below deck and left with water but no food.

On 2 May 1945, British troops commanded by Major-General George Roberts, discovered the Neuengamme camp. It was empty and had been cleaned up by the last prisoners. The British troops followed the trail of bodies and reached Lübeck which capitulated without a shot. Lübeck had suffered a single bombing raid on Palm Sunday, in 1942. After this, it had been appointed as a "Port of the International Red Cross" and under international rules, was never attacked again. It had a permanent Red Cross Office there, at this time under the charge of M de Blonay. He informed Major-General Roberts that over 8,000 concentration camp prisoners had recently been loaded onto the three ships in the Bay. This information was also presented to the British forces by a Swedish Red Cross delegate.

Before Hitler committed suicide on the 30th April 1945, he named his successor as Grand-Admiral Dönitz. Dönitz was astonished to find that he had been appointed as President of the Reich (not Führer, a title that Hitler wished to keep only to himself). Hitler also dismissed Himmler from the Nazi Party for treachery. However, Himmler saw himself, and was seen by many others, as Hitler's natural successor. He did not think the Reich could manage without him, so he ignored Hitler's edict. Dönitz's headquarters were at the Plön naval base, not far from the Bay of Lübeck. Himmler immediately visited Dönitz, taking with him an impressive and intimidating body of SS men and armoured troop carriers. Despite Hitler's dismissal, Dönitz agreed, in talks with Himmler, that he would have a role in the new government, although its precise nature was left open. Admiral Dönitz moved his headquarters to the nearby port of Flensburg, where more administrative space could be found. Himmler also moved his team there to make sure of keeping his jack-boots in the corridors of power. He was still hopeful that he could persuade Eisenhower and Churchill to join with Germany and defeat the Russians. (In this respect Himmler correctly foresaw the alliances of the subsequent Cold War.)

On 3 May 1945, on their way to Flensburg, Himmler's entourage was attacked by an RAF plane. The SS troops and office staff abandoned their vehicles and ran for shelter in the woods, all except for Himmler himself who stayed in his armour-plated Mercedes shouting for his men to come back. The RAF plane was presumably from one of the squadrons that had started the attack further south.

That same day, RAF aircraft from five squadrons attacked the ships in Lübeck Bay: the Cap Arcona, the Thielbeck and the Deutschland. The aircraft were RAF Hawker Typhoon fighter-bombers based in Ahlhorn, Hustedt and Wunstorf (near Hannover). They carried 20mm cannon, high explosive rockets and two 500 lb bombs. As the first attack started, the planes swooped over the unarmed ships firing cannons and rockets. All three ships were hit and fires started. The planes circled round and flew back to their bases to re-arm.

Adam Hamelmann was on the Cap Arcona at this time. His son Walter, who was 18, had been stationed just a week before, as a fresh conscript, in the army camp in Oldenburg, Holstein. He was given leave to visit his father and made his way to Neustadt. He could not have come at a worse time. He walked down to the beach and spotted a small launch which had just brought some wounded people to shore after the first air raid. The launch was on its way back to the Cap Arcona to rescue some more wounded people. Walter waved and called out. A sailor on board, recognized him as Adam's son: he knew him from the many visits he had made to his father when the ship was anchored in Gotenhafen. So he gave Walter a lift to the ship. The sailor was obviously trying to help but, with hind-sight, it is difficult to understand why he didn't realize the danger he was putting Walter (and himself) in. The ships had just suffered one attack by the RAF. Perhaps he thought the RAF would realize their attack was a mistake and call it off. After all, the Red Cross had been told of the situation and had passed it on to Major-General Roberts. Why would the British want to bomb ships carrying concentration camp prisoners?

Adam and Walter had very little time to greet each other and talk before a second wave of RAF Hawker Typhoons started their attack. The Cap Arcona was strafed and bombed. More fires broke out. Below deck there were thousands of concentration camp prisoners locked into the holds. There were no portholes, they were below the water line. Suddenly there was a loud explosion and the ship shuddered. They felt more explosions. The prisoners tried desperately to open the door by pounding it with a plank of wood. People were shouting and running outside in the corridors. The hold started to fill with smoke. The prisoners could hardly breathe, they were coughing, choking and very frightened. The ship was listing. Then the lights went out. The prisoners became absolutely terrified.

At last someone outside the hold unlocked the door and everyone rushed out to escape. They were three floors below the main deck. It was chaos. Prisoners ran up staircases only to find they were blocked by smoke and flames. In the sound and fury they ran this way and that in terror and panic. Some lucky people managed to reach the open deck. Nearby they could see the Thielbeck burning. The Deutschland was in flames and tipped on one side. It had a large Red Cross clearly visible on one of its funnels. The sea was full of people trying to swim to shore, a distance of about three kilometres. The water was cold and many were pulled down by the vortices caused by the sinking ship. There were also SS guards on the shore, shooting at swimmers in the water.

It was early afternoon. Another squadron of RAF planes appeared. The concentration camp victims, now on deck, could see their markings. They shouted with joy, "They're British! We're saved!" They waved their striped caps and indicated their striped concentration camp uniforms. They jumped and yelled but it had no effect. The airmen continued to fire cannons and drop bombs without restraint. The ship continued to burn and list until finally, it capsized and slowly sank down to the shallow bottom of the bay. Some of those on board escaped by jumping into the cold water wearing life-jackets, including most of the SS guards. Many without life-jackets also jumped into the water and started swimming to shore. RAF pilots had been told to shoot people in the water and they did so. The troops on the shore also continued firing their guns. There was nothing the swimmers could do to protect themselves. It was a blood bath; very few survived.

The Athen and some German fishing trawlers, at great risk to themselves, managed to save some of the crew and 350 of the 5,000 concentration camp victims. Benjamin Jacobs, was one of these survivors, rescued from the deck of the Cap Arcona onto a small boat. He describes his experience in graphic and first-hand detail in his book *The Dentist of Auschwitz*. The Thielbeck was also in flames: only 50 of the 2,800 prisoners on board were rescued. The Deutschland was luckier: before it capsized all 2,000 of the prisoners were rescued by the motor launch Athen. However, at the end, with the loss of an estimated 7,500 lives, this event goes down as one of the worst and cruellest disasters in naval history.

Why did it happen, despite the clear information given by the Red Cross to Major-General Roberts the previous day? It is possible that the information did not reach RAF Command in time. But they had radio communication: they didn't send a man on a horse to take the news, although there would have been time enough even for that. Why did the planes ignore the men in striped concentration camp uniforms shouting from the deck. Why did they ignore the clearly visible Red Cross painted on the funnel of the Deutschland? But, above all, why was the attack ordered at all? The group of SS High Command, including Himmler, had been spotted and attacked in their cars heading towards Flensburg which is right on the Danish border. The SS went there because it was the seat of the new Dönitz government. It has been proposed that they were planning to escape to Norway using the ships in the Lübeck Bay. Why would they risk their own lives to travel south from Flensburg and then board this flotilla of highly visible ships, full of thousands of prisoners to escape to Scandinavia? Himmler could have given orders for the three ships to set sail to Norway while they drove north through Denmark and then, with a short sea crossing, reached Norway far more securely. Both countries were still under German control.

It may have been that the rapid advance of the British troops north meant that the plans to transport and release the White Bus prisoners in Scandinavia had to be abandoned. This seems unlikely as all three of the ships were ready to go, although the Cap Arcona still had engine problems and could only cruise slowly. It has also been suggested that the SS were planning to scuttle the ships, sink them with U-boats or bomb them by the Luftwaffe in order to get rid of the evidence of concentration camp victims. But that creates a bizarre twist of logic. Firstly, they were too late to get rid of the evidence: the Allies had already opened the Gates of Hell in Bergen-Belsen and other concentration camps and had seen the horrors of themselves. Secondly, if Himmler had devoted so much time and effort to collect together all the "Aryan" prisoners in Neuengamme, so that they could be returned to Scandinavia and thus saved because they were part of the mythical "Master Race", then the three ships could have set off as soon as the Aryans were on board. Why would he change his mind and now want to murder them? There was no evidence that any action had been taken by the SS to scuttle or attack their own sitting-duck ships. Unbelievably and shamefully, the RAF did that instead.

Adam and Walter Hamelmann did not survive the RAF attack. Thousands of bodies were washed up on the beaches (and continued appearing, as body parts and bones, for many years afterwards). When they heard the news, Trudel Hamelmann and her brother, my father Maximilian, went to the Bay of Lübeck. They walked along the beaches, turning over bodies and searching for hours, looking for the body of Adam. (At that time they did not know that Walter had joined the ship, literally in its last hour.) It was a harrowing task. They did not find Adam among the thousands of bodies lying there. Trudel continued hoping to hear news from her son Walter into October of that year, 1945. She did not know what had happened to him but kept hoping he was still alive somewhere, perhaps as a prisoner of war.

One day Trudel met a women by chance at a station in Hamburg. She was a friend of the family and had discovered that Walter had gone to the ship on the day of the attack. She told Trudel what she knew: Walter must have lost his life on that fateful day. It was a tragedy none of the family could ever forget, especially Trudel, who had lost both her beloved husband and son just *one day* before the surrender of the German troops in northwest Germany, when all military action ceased. Werner, who had lost his father and brother, was also devastated. He collected photos and memorabilia of the Cap Arcona sinking and created a poignant display on a wall in his house. They continued to mourn the tragedy for many years.

There is a monument in Neustadt to the Cap Arcona and Thielbeck victims. Prisoners from over 30 nations, who died so cruelly and needlessly, are commemorated there. The RAF killed 7,500 helpless concentration camp victims and others on the ships. Jacobs and Pool in their book *"The Hundred Years Secret: Britain's Hidden World War II Massacre "* ask why the British Government locked the documents of this attack away for 100 years. Something to hide? Guilty consciences? No British government has ever explained why the RAF attacked the ships. They have not accepted responsibility for the massacre of all these helpless, innocent people or admitted that it was a terrible mistake. They have never laid a wreath at the Neustadt Memorial. It seems to be an act of denial that they were responsible for this disaster.

Memorial to the sinking of the Cap Arcona and the Thielbeck, 3 May 1945.

Chapter Fifteen

The War Ends

Nie wieder Krieg! (Never again War!) a grafitti
slogan painted up many places in Germany after the
war, including, very appropriately, on the podium used
by Hitler during the Nazi Rallies in Nuremberg.
It is often followed by: *Nie wieder Völkermord!*
(Never again Genocide!)

The Second World War was rapidly coming to an end.
Mussolini was captured by Italian Partisans and executed
on 28 April 1945. His body was then strung up from a
lamp post. The day after that, the German forces in Italy
surrendered. Russian forces had surrounded and entered
Berlin. Hitler married Eva Braun on 29 April and the following
afternoon, to escape Mussolini's fate, they committed suicide.
Under instruction, their bodies were burnt in the garden of
his bunker. The German forces in Berlin surrendered to the
Russian General Vasily Chuikov on 2 May 1945.

On 3 May, Gauleiter Kaufmann surrendered Hamburg
to the Allied troops without resistance. This meant it escaped

artilery bombardment and more deaths. Hitler had ordered that no town should surrender without a fight to the death. Kaufmann considered that Hitler had lost all sense of reality and ignored the edict. However he kept a constant bodyguard because, although Hitler was dead, there were still extremist Nazis who would shoot Kaufmann as a traitor.

On 4 May 1945, the day after the sinking of the Cap Arcona in Lübeck Bay, the German forces in northwest Germany surrendered unconditionally to Field Marshal Montgomery at Lüneburg. There is a slim possibility that the RAF attack in Lübeck Bay had helped to persuade the German forces to surrender, despite the fact that nearly all of the victims of this attack were concentration camp prisoners. But the mood had changed. German forces in the Netherlands, Denmark, Bavaria and central European countries surrendered soon after. V-E Day (Victory in Europe Day) was declared on 8 May 1945.

A couple of weeks before the sinking of the Cap Arcona, Allied forces moving north from the Normandy landings, encountered the Nazi concentration camp at Bergen-Belsen. They liberated it on 15 April 1945. In the camp were about 60,000 prisoners, starving and in unbelievably terrible condition. Heaps of dead bodies lay everywhere. The British commander ordered the SS guards to dig mass graves and bury the dead. Those still living were given water and fed as best as the troops could manage. Women from Oldendorf and the other surrounding villages were sent to the camp to help the victims. But it was too late for many of them, they died even as they were being helped. It was a sight that those who saw it could never forget.

Bergen-Belsen was a mere 10 km from Oldendorf where we were living and yet no one in the village seemed to know what was happening there. Prisoners and supplies were brought to Belsen by rail and not by road, where they might have been seen by villagers. The camp had no incinerators so there were no tell-tale plumes of smoke. However, apart from the SS guards, there must have been many people (including local people) involved in the running of the camp. Perhaps there were some who knew but were too scared to tell. I am convinced that most people in Oldendorf, and certainly my mother, knew nothing about it. She would have told us, not then of course, but later in life. We had long conversations about our time in Germany during the war, often asking specifically about Belsen. She would certainly have told us about the camp if she knew anything. It is still astounding to me that we were living "pretty idyllic" lives in a lovely village in beautiful countryside no more than a long walk away from that "Hell on Earth"!

*

Werner was still in an Allied PoW camp. One of the anecdotes he told us after his release was about the Austrian troops in the camp. After the Anschluss, Austrians had mostly regarded themselves as part of the German family. In the camp, however, they thought that, if they differentiated themselves from the Germans, they might be seen as less culpable for the horrors of the war and thus be better treated. (It should not be forgotten that Hitler was a "trumped-up Austrian corporal".) The Red Cross arrived with food parcels for the Germans. The Austrians held their ground: they did not admit to being Germans so they received no parcels.

At the end of the war, my father Maximilian, was given a job in the Hamburg Baupolizei (police building department) to find and authorize homes for displaced people in Hamburg. It was a difficult job because of the massive destruction Hamburg had suffered. The initial cleaning up after the Gomorrah bombing had been done by prisoners from the Neuengamme concentration camp. They had to find dead bodies, in whole or parts, and load them into lorries for burial in Ohlsdorf cemetery. They also cleared the streets of rubble to allow cars and lorries through. Walls that seemed precarious were demolished for safety. Restoration and building work was started not long after the German surrender. After the main clearance, the next stage was often done by organized groups of women who cleared huge numbers of bomb sites, brick by brick. Bricks that remained whole were assembled into neat stacks to be reused and the broken rubble was used for foundations or dumped elsewhere. In Berlin, where this also happened, a whole new hill was created out of war rubble.

[I remember in the summer of 1954 walking from Barmbek station to Richardstraße, where Trudel Hamelmann then lived, a distance of about 1.5 km. I walked through large areas where, northwest of the Hamburger Straße, there were barely any houses standing at all: just a few empty shells. Makeshift footpaths had developed across these bombed-out areas. But in some parts of the city, plain tall blocks of flats (Hochhäuser) were then being rapidly built to provide some accommodation for homeless people.]

In the Baupolizei our father had been given the perfect opportunity to find a home for himself, his wife and family. Through his job he was aware of all the rebuilding and conversion projects planned or underway around the city. However, he left us living on the farm in Oldendorf, coming down occasionally to see us. The war was over but we were still living as refugees in the Martens' farm house. They probably thought it was time for us to move back to Hamburg but they didn't put any pressure on us. They were very kind and caring people. It was Max's lack of urgency to get the family living together again that made our mother, in late 1945, explore the possibility of going back to England. She wrote to her brother Eric about it. Dolly and Max were very happy in the early years of their marriage when they lived in Hamburg but the separation and traumas of the war had made life very difficult for her. She was strong and stoical and looked after us children with unwavering love during the war years. But after the war, she was still bearing all the responsibility for us children and herself. I think Dolly still loved Maximilian but he seemed to make no moves to get his family back together again. Why, we shall never know.

After a long period of mourning for the death of her husband Adam and son Walter on the Cap Arcona, Tante Trudel started thinking about finding a new home. In December 1945 she wrote that she had collected enough furniture for her own apartment. Although, at first, she had found it easy to stay in a large house with friends or relatives, she now wanted to find a place for herself and Opa, ready for when Werner was released from his PoW camp. Trudel then fell out with the Krügers (in Hamburg's Hoheneichen suburb) so, in early 1946, her search for a new home became more urgent. "Better a small home for her family than sharing with strangers in a large house." Her motto was "klein aber mein" "small but mine". Trudel went to Lustadt in the Pfalz to fetch Opa Max. Back in Hamburg she visited Else and Richard Koschel, for the first time since they got back from Krakau. They had found a new apartment in Finkenau 30. Rosi was also there with her young son Klaus who was a "ray of sunshine". Very sadly, Rosi's husband Günter Uttermann, had left her. Due to the war, they had barely had any significant peroid of married life together. Trudel wrote that "it was the duty of every married man to take responsibility for the care of his family." She probably tried to impress that on our father, Maximilian, as well.

On the first anniversary of the sinking of the Cap Arcona, Trudel was still looking for a home. In June, Max found an attic for sale in Richardstraße. (This was just a short walk from her sister Else Koschel and family in their new apartment.) Maximilian thought it would be suitable but it needed building work to convert it into apartments. It was for sale so, if they could raise the money, they would not have to pay rent every month. It took the combined savings of Max, Trudel and Opa to buy it, which they did in July 1946. They brought in professional workmen but they all helped with the rebuilding as well. It was an open attic space over a large apartment block, big enough to accomodate four reasonably large apartments. They started building internal walls; meanwhile doors and windows were delivered.

Trudel started to search for furniture for their new home. She found a very nice sideboard in a furniture shop and reserved it for when the apartment would be ready. Later she discovered that it had been sold to someone else which made her very cross. Trudel writes frequently to Werner in his PoW camp:

(29.7.1946): Recently I have been looking for new kitchen furniture. I found a very nice little kitchen cooker and a [typical German] tiled stove which was installed in the sitting room. It will all be lovely when you get here. It is extraordinary, whole families are now homeless. Most of them are Nazis and God knows that we are not! Party members are on their heels, they have nothing to laugh about any more. It's good that we never had anything to do with them!

We have just received a parcel from Sweden from a friend of Opa Max. In it there was 1 lb coffee, 1 lb cocoa, 1/2 lb tea, maize, porridge oats, flour, two tins of sardines in oil and two packets of cheese. Wonderful! I can't tell you how much Opa and I were delighted with it. We won't go hungry. In any case, I can always find places to buy enough food.

Trudel looked forward so much to Werner being with her in their own home again. She and Opa were still staying with friends, the Krügers, in the beautiful suburbs of Hamburg. At the end of July she wrote to Werner:

(30.7.1946): When you get out of the PoW camp, perhaps soon after, you will want to get married and then I shall be on my own again. Sometimes I am worried about that, but if it must be, so be it. We can still look forward to the indescribable joy of having our own home again. Every day brings our goal nearer. However, my health is suffering from this constant feeling of dependency (on the Krügers). It destroys my soul to be called every day to task and I have done nothing more than sacrifice everything for this war. Those who have been spared by this terrible war don't feel sympathy for us. On the contrary, they think that no one is so loud, inconsiderate and unclean as we bombed-out folk. I slink around the house like a thief so that no one can hear me. I sleep until nine in the mornings and keep quiet. I sleep again at noon and have to stay quiet. After 10 in the evening, no more sound must be heard from us. But at last a golden freedom is coming and I won't need to humiliate myself any more. I haven't written this to you before, my Werner, because I didn't want to give you a heavy heart. But soon I'll have my own kitchen with a sink and gas-cooker. There are still many things to be done to get this home finished. But it should all be done by September.

Trudel's letter to Werner in August describes their progress:

(5.8.1946): We are still working hard on the apartment. it is truly satisfying because there is such a strong sense of purpose behind it. I feel lucky that in these pleasing rooms we will be able to heal ourselves from the terrible years of war and have our two beloved dead (Adam and Walter) always in our memory. You could train as an architect which Hamburg desperately needs. You can rely on my support.

Werner had still not been released from the PoW camp, although many others had already gone home. Trudel made an application for his release (19.8.1946). She hoped the PoW camp officers will be reasonable as she has already suffered enough from this war. Trudel wrote, "Don't they know how heavy a burden it is on a mother's heart? I look forward to us sitting comfortably in our own home with the men playing cards, or you (Werner) telling us the tales of your time in the war." She also wrote, perhaps with more hope than expectation, "Dolly will go back to London shortly with her children and Max will follow soon after."

Trudel writes to Werner again a couple of days later:

(21.9.1946): The attic will be divided into four apartments. The bricklayer will finish the first one this week, his own, and ours will be the next one. We hope to move in by the end of September. I will no longer be dependent on the kindness of friends. We'll have our own kitchen and you can help me sometimes with the drying up.

Werner replies with a short letter in late August, saying that, if nothing goes wrong, his group will shortly be moving to a PoW camp in Germany. He recently "celebrated" his second anniversary as a prisoner of war and this long period of separation which has brought him so much sadness and pain. For some unexplained offence, he has had his head shaved as a punishment and will be coming home with a crew cut. But it will grow again. He wonders if the new apartment will be ready when he gets home. He praises Trudel for her amazing achievements (25.8.1946).

However, the apartment is still not ready. The bricklayer reckons it will take another 14 days. Trudel writes to Werner about progress and her misgivings about my father:

(26.8.1946): Unfortunately, we must include Maximilian as a buyer, as he is the legal originator (Urheber) of the purchase. However, I hope he takes your example to be friendly and shows respect towards me. We will live here rent-free for ten years. There are two big rooms and Max gets the small bedroom. There is a large bathroom but the kitchen could be bigger. The sitting room may not always be as warm as we would like because there is so little fuel available these days. We have lost so much in this war. I hope you can come home soon. You are the one person who really understands me. Opa is too old to understand me fully, he is already 87. At the end of this week we can start painting the apartment. I have not given up on that sideboard that was taken from me. I will not give up until I get it."

The last few letters arrived from Werner. "They are moving us to a PoW camp in Munster, which is just a short step from release. One transport has already gone, it must be our turn soon. Visitors are permitted in Munster. Perhaps two more days; hope is rising in the camp!" His last letter was sent from the Munster PoW camp. He has received three letters from Trudel which were sent via Belgium. So his PoW camp was not in France as they had thought but somewhere in Belgium. His final words from the camp are:

(14.9.1946): I can hardly believe that the day we have been longing for with impatience for so long is almost here. From the bottom of my heart I am so thankful that we shall be together again soon. The pain of our heavy losses will weigh upon us and make us sad when we think of them. But then we will not be alone any more, we will understand and support each other. Why should we not be happy again? I know that the conditions in Germany will make life hard but you are my model. I have learnt from you that everything is possible and nothing is fruitless. One must have courage and confidence even when your heart is almost breaking. Life will be better for us again. I have faith in the future."

In late September 1946, Werner was finally released from his PoW camp after being held for over two years. Despite what he went through in the war, he still seems optimistic about the future. He was sent twice to Russia, shot through the shoulder and lung on the second occasion, had painful months of convalescence. He spent time in Norway, was on the train journey with the crash in Belgium. Had the long march through Belgium and France and was finally captured with the fake Francs and then spent two years in an Allied PoW camp. Many people of his parent's generation had now witnessed Germany crushed and destroyed twice in 30 years, suffering hyperinflation between the two wars. They had seen the rise and fall of fascism. It takes a rare person to feel positive about the future after all that.

At last Werner arrived in Hamburg and moved into the new apartment. What a tearful, joyful reunion that must have been

Hamburg 1946, Trudel, Werner, Rosi, Opa Max, Klaus held in front of Maximilian by Richard Koschel, Else Koschel.

after all the years of uncertainty and loss. Trudel had endured the deaths her husband Adam and her younger son Walter in the sinking of the Cap Arcona. She blessed the day when her elder, beloved son Werner, was allowed to return to her. There were still a few jobs left to finish in the apartment but it was perfectly habitable. After two years of enforced idleness or pointless labour in PoW camps, Werner was allowed to have his life back again.

So what was Werner's attitude to life after being a soldier in the war and then a prisoner of war? Was he a broken man? On the contrary, when he got back to Hamburg, he set to work with a new sense of purpose. He designed and installed a wonderful modern bathroom in Trudel's flat in which all the plumbed items were connected into a smooth curved painted plywood structure that he constructed. It looked very smart and modern. He then went on to study architecture. He married Henny and built his own lovely modern house In Ahrensburg, a town a short distance north of Hamburg. They had three boys Achim, Walter and Martin. He also studied carpentry and created a business importing household furniture from Denmark, keeping in touch with our Mikkelsen relatives there. The demand for furniture increased as the rebuilding of houses accelerated in Germany. I never heard a word of self-pity from him despite his terrible injury and near-death experiences in Russia during the war.

Our father, Maximilian stayed on in the new apartment and made no moves to find a home for us, his family. He continued to annoy Trudel by coming home late at night, usually drunk.

Richard, Klaus and Maximilian Barth in Hamburg 1946.

Chapter Sixteen

We Move to England

It was 1946, the war was over and we were still living in Oldendorf as refugees. We often asked about our Papa: when is he coming here or when are we going to join him in Hamburg? Our mother, Dolly, had been writing to her family in England. She told her brother, Eric Shaw, that life was hard and made all the harder as Max showed no sign of wanting to find us a home with him in Hamburg.

Eric Shaw ran an antiques shop in Brighton at 109 Western Road. His business was going quite well. Brighton was noted for antiques shops in those days, especially in "The Lanes". At that time people didn't have a lot of money but, with men returning from the war, they started moving into new homes and needed furniture and fittings. His shop didn't just have antiques but it included all sorts of household items. Before the war Eric had a business making modern lampshades for Heals in London. He had a wide range of practical skills and could turn his hand to anything. He also had a good eye for picking up furniture and other items in auctions and "junk shops", repairing them or converting them into something that people needed in that post-war period. He took unwanted wardrobes, turned the main section through 90°, put it on a plinth, added shelves and doors, covered the top with formica and thus created a very desirable modern kitchen unit.

Eric had started investigating the possibilities of getting his sister Dolly and us children to England many months before. After a lot of form-filling, he obtained the necessary permission on condition that he would give an assurance that we "would not be a financial burden on the State." With fingers crossed, I guess, he gave that assurance. The bureaucracy was completed and the travel arrangements made. In the farmhouse in Oldendorf, late December 1946, we packed up our few possessions. We had been living with the Martens family in Oldendorf for over two years. They had been very good to us, taking us in as refugees from bombed-out Hamburg. We were not related but they had always treated us like family. We said our goodbyes with many hugs and tears. (We kept in touch and in the summer of 1953, Herr and Frau Martens came over and visited us in England.)

A pick-up truck turned up at the door of the farmhouse. It was an open truck, half full of split logs. We climbed aboard and sat where we could, the logs were hard and uncomfortable. However, this was no ordinary wood delivery truck: the logs were also the fuel. It was powered by a Stirling external combustion engine, similar to a steam engine. The driver stoked the small boiler and off we went to Hamburg, a journey of about 100 km. We were well wrapped up but it was still a very cold journey.

We stayed for two or three days in Trudel's new flat in Richardstraße with our father Max, grandfather (Opa Max) and Trudel's son, Werner. Trudel and Werner were happily reunited after the long cruel years of war. We were shown round all the work they had done to create their own home again. It was very cosy. Our mother must have thought that if Max could put so much money, time and effort into creating such a splendid apartment for his sister, father and nephew, he might have done the same for his own wife and children! Shouldn't we actually come first? When it was time to go to the docks for our trip to England, Max took us there on the U-Bahn (Hamburg's light railway). He said goodbye to us on the station platform, from where we could see many ships in the docks. We wondered when we would see him again.

Dolly, Annemarie and I boarded a British troop-carrier ship going from Hamburg to Hull. It was taking home soldiers who had completed their spell of duty in Germany. Sailing down the Elbe towards the North Sea there was a jolly atmosphere on board ship: the men were looking forward to getting back home. They were very friendly to us children even though we only spoke German.

On board ship, we had a cabin to ourselves. There were two bunks and I shared the top bunk with Annemarie. It was possible to look out of the porthole from there. When we got out to sea, I started feeling seasick and spent most of my time in the bunk suffering nausea and looking out of the porthole. On one occasion I famously said, "What a lot of water!!" which made my mother laugh. The Alster in Hamburg was the largest stretch of water I had ever seen until then. I did not know that there were seas and oceans where land was not visible in any direction.

Our poor mother also suffered from seasickness but Annemarie was fine, she wandered around the ship and talked to people. She met a WAAF woman and made friends with her. On one visit to her cabin, Annemarie hung back a bit as the metal door shut. It caught and sliced her finger so that the top it was hanging off. Dolly was called from her bunk to find Annemarie crying in great pain. She asked for the doctor who was called from *his* bed. He took Annemarie to the surgery and sewed the top of her finger back on again. She was left with a permanent scar but didn't lose any of her finger.

After two days we docked at Hull and caught a train to London. A lady in the carriage opposite us kindly offered Annemarie and me a banana each. We had never seen one before, there were none in Germany during the war. Our mother passed one to Annemarie and then peeled one for me. Not realizing, Annemarie bit straight into hers without peeling it. Oooh, it was so tough and bitter! I bit into my peeled one and ate a mouthful. Wow, it was delicious! Annemarie's experience put her off bananas completely. I tried to persuade her that they were great but she wouldn't relent. I think it was several years before she ate her first banana.

When we reached London, we went to stay with Aunty Gretchen, Dolly's sister, in their flat in Regent's Square. Gretchen was married to Johnny Cantor, a violinist, who ran a popular jazz band for many years before the war. After the war he played violin in several London orchestras. They had two children, David and Anne, who were twins a couple of years younger than me. We stayed for two or three nights in London so that Dolly and Gretchen could have a long talk about what had happened to them both during the ten years they had been apart. We children played together perfectly happily, as children do, despite not sharing a common language.

The final leg of our journey was by train down to Brighton. Uncle Eric met us at the station and took us to his antiques shop. There was a significant amount of living space above the shop. On the first floor, at the back, was a small kitchen, dining room and bedroom. At the front over the shop, there was a large studio-cum-sitting room. The second floor had another large studio with a bedroom and bathroom behind. This was to be our new home. Anna and I slept in a large four-poster bed which was actually part of the stock of the shop: it could have been sold from under us any day. It seemed absolutely vast to us. I remember one night our mother read us a bed-time story from "Peter Pan". She had reached the chapter about Peter and Wendy being captured by pirates and chased by crocodiles. It gave me such a nightmare that I fell out of bed. The floor was a long way down.

Eric had a daily help called Midge who came in every day to cook and clean for him. My mother was now perfectly willing and able to take on these jobs but, perhaps from loyalty, Eric kept Midge on. I called her "lovely Midge" because she was so kind and welcoming to us and fed us little treats. Eric also had many friends who popped in to see him. Annemarie and I were well brought-up German children so when we were introduced to someone, we would shake hands; Annemarie would do a little curtsy and I would bow my head and click my heels. This was the accepted custom in Germany but it didn't take us long to realize that this was not normal practice in England and we were, in fact, objects of some harmless amusement to visitors. So quite soon after this, Anna gave up the curtsy and I stopped the heel-clicking. It was a shame really: the loss of a sign of respect, although I have to admit, I never took it up again.

We often asked our mother when Papa would join us in England. She told us that he couldn't come now because he had been a soldier in the German Army and "had to be forgiven first. But Germany is kaputt, life is not good there anymore. I hope he will come to England for a better life very soon." Annemarie and I had to be satisfied with that.

As it was getting close to Christmas, Uncle Eric devised a money-raising scheme to buy us presents. When any of his many friends visited, he asked if they would like to pay "A Shilling to see the Darlings." That was us two, young blond children asleep in the four-poster bed. The visitors didn't disurb us and we had no idea it was happening.

On Christmas morning, after breakfast, Uncle Eric took us all into the first floor studio. There was a Hornby "O" gauge LMS Princess Elizabeth 6201 electric train on a track lay-out, which filled most of the room. It also had various waggons connected to it. Wow!! I had never seen anything like it. Uncle Eric got the train going, changed the points, showed me how the speed could be controlled, how it could be sent anywhere on the lay-out, stopped, reversed and so on, using the transformer controls. "Have a go, Peter." So I did. It was the most amazing and exciting toy I had ever played with in my life! Annemarie had a go too, then my mother. When it was time to stop, I asked if I might be allowed to play with it again the next day. Uncle Eric said, "Of course. It's your Christmas present!" I had absolutely no idea! It was inconceivable to me that this was now mine. I had grown up with the expectation that Christmas presents would be a handful of nuts, some fruit or a piece of cake and perhaps a knitted scarf or gloves. Uncle Eric had collected up the "Darling's Shillings" which contributed a little to the cost of the train set which he bought at an auction. What a wonderful present. What a wonderful uncle!

We lived for about a year under Uncle Eric's roof (and feet) in his antiques shop. Annemarie and I were sent to school in the first term of 1947 to the nearby Roman Catholic primary school, St Mary Magdalene's. At the time, we couldn't speak or understand much English. We were in different class rooms and when I got confused or worried, I would ask if Anna could come and help me sort it out. It was very reassuring to have my big sister close. One of the things that worried and frightened me was being called a Nazi. I didn't know what it meant but it was clearly something very Nasty. We spent the first two terms of 1947 at that school and then came the summer holidays.

Brighton beach in the summer was a paradise for us children. It was just a short walk down the hill from the antiques shop. Our mother took us down there on sunny days, sometimes with Uncle Eric's black and tan dachshund, Max, cheekily but affectionately named after our father. Although neither of us could swim at that time, there was plenty to do and other children to play with. The dog would find a stone and then spend a lot of time apparently blunting his teeth on it. We would throw it for him to retrieve on a beach of nothing but stones, but he would always find his special stone and bring it back. At low tide when the sand appeared, which didn't coincide witth our visits very often, we could go shrimping and catch a few for tea, but mostly, I let them go: it didn't seem fair.

If we had been very good, we were given an ice-cream from the kiosk on the seafront. Sometimes we walked along to the the West Pier which was beautiful and totally intact in those days. There was a paddling pool nearby which was great for the very young to get used to being in the water. When the Punch and Judy show was going by the pier, we watched it with great excitement.

In a few months we were speaking and understanding child-level English pretty well. Our grandmother, Emilie Shaw, who had moved to Hove by then, insisted that our mother and Eric should speak to us only in English. She wanted the German expunged as soon as possible. However, if we didn't understand, of course they had to speak to us in German and then in English as well. Children's brains are conditioned to learn languages quickly. In less than a year, we had switched to English completely. Annemarie and I have always regretted that we didn't continue speaking German because we forgot it almost completely in a couple of years. We had to relearn it later in life.

At the start of the new school year In September 1947, Annemarie and I were moved to Middle Street School, which was a little bit further away but had a much better reputation. Also, not being a religious school, we didn't have the frequent Saint's Days holidays. But most importantly, we were sufficiently fluent in English by then to make new friends who didn't call us Nazis. We no longer seemed so foreign to our contemporaries. Annemarie was advised to avoid her full name and only call herself Anna for the same reason.

Towards the end of 1947, Uncle Eric found us a basement flat in a beautiful Regency terraced house, 5 Norfolk Terrace, just two streets up the hill from his shop on the Western Road. The house had belonged to Ralph, a friend of Eric. He had just sold it to Mr Joscelyne who made a very profitable living in Billingsgate Fish Market in London. Ralph offered to find tenants for him. We went to see it one dark winter's evening. Most of the woodwork was painted brown and the lower part of the walls were dark green gloss making the place very gloomy. We found it rather depressing. It had been the kitchen and scullery of the main house upstairs and these were the standard downstairs colours of the time. It even had a disused dumb-waiter shaft which I later climbed up a few times.

The multi-talented Uncle Eric was soon painting and decorating the flat. The woodwork and much of the walls he painted white which brightened it all up. He quickly transformed it into a very nice flat. The semi-basement had a yard and steps up to the street at the front, while at the back there were rockery slopes covered with ferns and London Pride with steps leading to the garden. This was our new home which we found very exciting. We hadn't had our own home since we were bombed out of our apartment in Hamburg in July 1943 which, by then, I could only vaguely remember.

*

Annemarie and I continued to ask our mother if there was any news from our father and when was he coming to England. I had a particularly vivid dream one night. Maximilian went to the west coast of Germany and walked to the top of a high hill. There was a strong wind blowing. He had an umbrella which he opened and then held up high. Suddenly the wind caught it and up he went and flew all the way across the sea to England. (I didn't know about Mary Poppins at that time.) I think the story came into my dream because I was subconsciously willing our father to join us in our new home in England.

Meanwhile Max was getting on with his life in a more practical manner, without a brolly. He left the Baupolizei, Police

Building Department, at the end of April 1947, feeling unsuited to that sort of career. He had found a new job in the firm of Johannes Schüll, coffee-roasters. During a three month trial contract with them as manager, he came across a special tobacco-cutting machine. The machine was so brilliantly engineered that it outshone any competitors. Max saw an opportunity and negotiated a sole rights contract to sell them. For the remainder of his time with this firm, he sold them so successfully that he and Schüll made a lot of money. Max was selling them so fast that the delivery firm and manufacturer could not keep up with the demand. He had "tasted blood", that is, he enjoyed being back in business again! At the end of his contract with Schüll he contacted the firm of Erdmann Fischer who were the manufacturers of the brilliant machine. He got on very well with Erdmann and was offered a favourable contract as sales manager. Max continued to earn good money from selling the machines and was able to pay off a loan from his brother-in-law, Richard Koschel. He also ordered himself a fine new made-to-measure suit and a winter coat for November.

All this story came out from a letter (24.10.1947) from Max to our mother Dolly and us. Max was often overcome with an "overpowering longing" to come to England or for us to go back to Hamburg. We had been apart for ten months by this time and he wanted us to be together again. He often wondered if it had been the right thing to do: to let us go so easily. He thinks that our mother is working too hard in England and wonders if she has financial worries. He writes that he can help her now as his salary is very good (5,000 Marks per month). However, I think our mother did not get any money from Max to support his family. For the first year, living over the antiques shop, we were supported by her brother, Eric. Money was always very tight but she received no money from the state which was, after all, a condition of our permission to come to England. Soon after we moved to Norfolk Terrace, Dolly became the caretaker of the flats for a reduction in our rent. She was paid to clean the flat when tenants left and then to advertise for a new tenants. We had a lodger and when we got older, our mother worked as a night nurse in various nearby nursing homes in Hove and the lodger was, in effect, our baby sitter. Max was right: she *was* working too hard.

In his letters, Max wants to know how we are getting on at school in England. He is worried that we will forget our German and then only half-learn English. He is very proud of Annemarie who is "tall and beautiful with pure skin, a symmetrical face and really beautiful blue eyes. Oh Momma, how I envy you having the children." Then he asks about me. Was I all right after having had my tonsils out? (The operation had gone well.) He asks about the problem of my squint. It had developed suddenly during the second Gomorrah attack (27/28 July 1943) when the RAF bombed Hamburg and we were sheltering in the church crypt (Chapter 6). Max asks whether my squint has got better of its own accord. He writes, " Do not neglect it until this problem has been completely eliminated. Such a fault would be a handicap for the rest of his life. How is he developing? He is a clever boy. Is he still so soft and sensitive? Does he still cry so easily? Even so, I love the little chap and would do much to have him with me. Give him a kiss and a hug and say it comes from me."

My mother had already taken me to the Eye Hospital in Brighton at the time of this letter. I was taken through tests which consisted of looking through the two eyepieces of a machine in which I saw a bird and a cage. I had to turn a knob until the bird looked to me to be in the cage. Then it was switched to a trapese artist who had to be put on his trapese and so on. There were various other versions of the game which presumably measured the angle of the squint. Some months later, when I was seven, I was taken in for surgery by Mr Thorne-Thorne. I woke up with my left eye bandaged and after a couple of days was deemed ready to see the world again in a new way: I had 3D vision again!

I had to wear glasses for a couple of years after the operation, to complete the process of adjustment but the operation was completely successful and has remained so for the rest of my life. Wearing glasses led to my being called "Four-eyes" at school, but it didn't bother me at all: I could see properly again and that was all that mattered!

Another letter came from Max, sent on 28 November 1947. He thanks our mother for a parcel she had sent to him, full of various food items, including a pot of strawberry jam, which he had specially asked for. It seems however that the parcel had been tampered with. Tea and sugar were scattered, an envelope containing a letter from Annemarie had been torn open (had there been money in it?) and there were no cigarettes (were they sent?). Max bemoans the state Germany is in. "There is no honesty here any more." He also thanks our mother for the big parcel that arrived earlier, exactly on Trudel's birthday (9th November). That parcel contained coffee, cigarettes, chocolate, cocoa and other items including a fur coat and cap for Trudel's birthday. She was amazed and delighted. There was also a wonderful pair of boots for little Klaus (now 3 years old). The Koschels happened to be there with Klaus when the parcel arrived. He says that they will write to express their happiness and gratitude. Looking back, it's difficult to see how our mother could have afforded all these presents. I think her brother Eric, who was always very generous, must have helped.

In the same letter Max writes how busy he is now. He even works on his typewriter all day on Sundays. This is when, surprisingly, he feels at his best. He notices from Annemarie's little letter that she seems to be losing her ability to write good German, her spelling and grammar are both faulty. He worries again that we children will forget our German (which, unfortunately, we did) and not learn English properly (which we did). He thinks that the letters between him and Dolly have got "very tired". He suggests they should both take more trouble.

"We belong to each other and so we must write very regularly." He thinks it would be difficult for him to come to England. He has a well-paid job in which he is very happy. He will be 48 years old next month and, although he still feels like a young man, it would be very hard for him to start again in another (still hostile) country. However, he is going to do a six-month English language course and if we are still in England next summer, he will come over for four weeks.

Maximilian suffers a huge longing to be with his family again. He writes, "For the first time I realize the value of having a family, a wife and such dear children. Often I have reproached myself that I let you go away so easily." He asks again about how his children are developing. "How is Annemarie progressing at school? She needs to be tidy and diligent, with an outstanding character. If she turns out like her mother, I will be happy and contented. I have no worries about Peterle. He is thoughtful and has it in him. With his tranquility he will reach his goal." He asks about the squint in my eye and Annemarie's teeth. He hopes that we will write to him, in English if we find it easier. That was the last letter from him that we still possess.

One day in August of the following year, 1948, our mother told Annemarie and me that she had received a letter from Tante Trudel. It was about our father Max. She had received the letter about three weeks before, but it had taken her that long to screw up the courage to tell us. The news from Trudel was that our father had died, on the 19th of July 1948. We stood, all three of us, in the sitting room of Norfolk Terrace, arms around each other, crying our eyes out for a long time. The hope that out father would come and join us in England, especially now we had our own flat, was shattered for ever. We asked how he had died. Our mother said vaguely, it was something to do with his heart.

I did not hear the full story of how our father had died until many years later. In April 1978 I made a visit to Hamburg between two scientific meetings, one in Berlin and the other in

Sønderborg, Denmark. Hamburg was conveniently between the two venues. I stopped there for a two day visit and was invited to supper with some of the relatives. At some point in the evening, Trudel took me aside and after a short conversation about how we were all doing, she asked me if I knew how my father had died. I said our mother had told us it may have been a heart attack. Trudel obviously thought it was about time I learnt the truth. She told me that Max had come home late, drunk as usual. He had gone into the kitchen to make himself some coffee, put some water in the kettle, turned on the gas and struck a match. In his drunken state he failed to light the gas and failed to notice it hadn't lit. The match dropped to the floor and went out. He took a piece of cheese from the fridge and went back into his little bedroom which was immediately behind the kitchen. With his door open, he sat on the bed eating the cheese waiting for the kettle to boil. Under the combined effects of alcohol and gas, he passed out. In the morning Trudel awoke to a strong smell of gas. She went to the kitchen and, realizing that gas was coming out of the hob, turned it off immediately. Then she quickly opened all the windows in the apartment and the outside door. Werner and Opa, in the back bedroom, also opened their window. Coal-gas was highly toxic in those days (it included carbon monoxide) but luckily, all three of them survived because, during the night, there were closed doors between them and the kitchen. Max was found with his door open, slumped on the bed with his piece of cheese, dead. There was no note or any other indication that he may have committed suicide (which probably passed through their minds).

Trudel received a condolence letter (20.7.1948) from Maximilian's employer, Erdmann Fischer. He writes that he is surprised and perplexed about the tragic death of his colleague, Maximilian Barth. It is inconceivable to him that Max's death had anything to with the business because it was going so well. He describes him as an exceedingly industrious and willing worker. He will miss Herr Barth in the further development of their enterprise. He sends sympathy for Trudel's grievous loss.

Taking this together with his loving and caring letters to us in England (above), it seems that Maximilian was in a good job, earning very well and with good prospects. He loved his family, wanted to be together with us again somehow but felt he was too old to start a new life in England. There were no reasons for, or indications of, despair that might have led him to suicidal thoughts. On the contrary, he was doing very well. Trudel concluded it was a drunken accident. But she was shocked and furious with him: he could have killed them all! They had luckily escaped death during the bombing of Hamburg. Werner had faced death many times in Russia and elsewhere during his war service years. Having their lives imperilled now by her brother infuriated her. I realized that Trudel could never forgive Max for his drunken carelessness.

He died in the early hours of the 19th of July 1948. Maximilian Rudolf Franz Barth was cremated and his ashes placed with the other Barth family remains in Ohlsdorf Cemetery in Hamburg. He is in the company of the remains of the approximately 45,000 people who had died in the bombing of Hamburg five years earlier in July 1943.

Acknowledgements

This book would have been impossible to write without the collection of letters, the majority written by my cousin Werner Hamelmann, which were assiduously collected by his mother, Trudel, throughout the war years. However, I was not aware of their existence when I first started writing this book. My first efforts were based on six 90 minute cassette recordings I had made of conversations, firstly with my mother Dolly and sister Annemarie. Then, when we made a visit to Werner and his wife Henny in Fischen, Bavaria in 2002 and again in 2005 (when my mother was 99!) I took the opportunity to capture on tape some of Werner's tales of his war experiences. He was a great raconteur, always colourful and interesting, creating almost cinematic visions of events. I started writing up some of Werner's taped war stories in the context of our family's oral history. I also had letters, photographs and rough notes of conversations.

But there were too many unknowns, so not long after I had started, I got in touch with Werner's eldest son Achim and his wife Uta. They told me that Henny had a collection of Werner's letters which she had started typing into a computer. They had been beautifully written by Werner but the script was difficult to read. Achim and Uta continued the arduous work of transcribing all the letters that Trudel had collected from Werner, into a computer thus making them accessible to other readers. There were also letters from Trudel's husband Adam and other friends and members of the family, including a few from my father and mother. It was a long and difficult job. Achim and Uta sent me this file which contains over 450 letters: it is called Feldpost 1940-1946 (and remains their copyright). Suddenly an Aladdin's cave opened before me. I discovered details of what and where things had happened to our family during the war years, as revealed by these letters. I thank Achim and Uta profusely for access to this file. Only later did I discover that Achim Hammelmann, had published over half of these letters in an eBook by neobooks.com called „Ich bin jetzt Soldat, 1942-46, das Leben einer Familie aus Hamburg in 280 Briefen."

I would also like to thank Martin Hammelmann, Werner's youngest son, who gave me valuable information about the sinking of the Cap Arcona, based on what his father, Werner, had told him.

Klaus Melchers, born Uttermann during the flight of the Koschel family from Krakau as the Red Army moved west in December 1944, has been an enormous help to me. He is an inveterate archivist and has sent me huge files of photos and documents. Based on guesswork, I first wrote in Chapter 12 "Fleeing from Krakau", that the Koschels had taken two or three weeks to get back to Hamburg. Klaus emailed and phoned me up and gently explained that I had "got it all wrong." He directed me to the digitized copy of his mother's diary of 1945, which I had not spotted in the vast collection of material he had sent me. It had, in fact, taken the Koschel family almost a year to return to their home! The diary showed how close they had come to being caught twice in the bombing of Dresden: on 13 February and then in the attack on the docks on 16 April 1945. They also very narrowly missed being caught in the massacre in Aussig on 31 July 1945. They led charmed lives and got home safely to Hamburg at the end of 1945.

My sister Annemarie (married name, Appleton) is two and a half years older than me, so her memories of events in Germany are clearer than mine. Many of the reminiscences of life in Oldendorf (Chapter 13) and elsewhere were expanded, enriched and corrected by her. We had long discussions about our time there. She has been a great support to me throughout the whole process of writing this book.

My old (long-standing) friend Gerd Tschöpe, mentioned towards the end of Chapter 2, gave me the story of his father (Karl-Heinz) returning to Hamburg seriously wounded at the end of the war. Gerd became an English teacher, probably as a result of his visits to us in Brighton every summer from 1955 onwards. Gerd went through my manuscript and found errors that everyone else had missed: the eagle-eye of a great English teacher. He also corrected my German in places. The German version of my poem "Gomorrah" at the end of Chapter 6 was first translated by Gerd Tschöpe and me. However, I would like to thank Bettina Melchers (Klaus Melchers' daughter) who transformed it into beautiful poetic German, far better than my original.

Unexpected help came from a relative I didn't know I had: Hans-Ole Mørk. He made email contact with me after I had been searching genealogical sites online for links to my Danish grandmother, Ane Marie Mikkelsen. Her brother, Hans-Ole Mikkelsen, was the grandfather of Hans-Ole Mørk, so we are second cousins. He very kindly sent me information and photographs of our grandparents in Klovborg, Denmark. We discussed the Koschel family: we even had copies of exactly the same photgraphs of them in Grömitz and Krakau. He also kindly directed me to an online site about aircraft accidents in France which contained the details of Edgar Koschel's fatal crash in December 1942 (Chapter 7).

I would also like to thank my old friend and academic colleague, Nigel Grinter, who read my book in February 2020 on a visit back to this country. I gave him version 5 which was the latest then but just over half its present size. He found it difficult to follow relationships between the people in the stories and wanted to know more about what sort of people they were: useful comments. I added the family trees page and gave a fuller picture of the members of my family.

Thanks are also due to Jan Bengree, who is a member of the Chester Little Theatre, an amateur theatre which Jane and I belong to. She runs a writing group and gave me helpful encouragement to start this book.

Lastly, but certainly most importantly, is the help I have had from my wife, Jane (who I first met on Brighton beach). She has a B.A. in English Language and Literature (Liverpool University) and practised her art as a teacher of English and Drama in a local secondary school near us in Cheshire. Apart from discussing every aspect of the book with me, she has gone through it with her fine toothcomb, many times, to improve every aspect of my English usage and story telling. Any infelicities or errors remaining are entirely my own responsibility.

Bibliography

Paddy Ashdown, *Nein*, London, William Collins, 2018.

Hector Bolitho, *A Summer in* Germany, London, Oswald Wolff, 1963.

Achim Hammelmann, *Ich bin jetzt Soldat, 1942-46, das Leben einer Familie aus Hamburg in 280 Briefen*, neobooks.com eBooks.

Benjamin Jacobs, *The Dentist of Auschwitz: A Memoir*, University Press of Kentucky, 1995

Benjamin Jacobs and Eugene Pool: *The Hundred Years Secret: Britain's Hidden World War II Massacre*, The Lyons Press, 2004.

Keith Lowe, *Inferno, the Devastation of Hamburg, 1943*, London, Penguin Books, 2012.

Neil MacGregor, *Germany, Memories of a Nation*, London, Allen Lane, Penguin, 2014.

Mark Mazower, *Hitler's Empire*, London, Penguin Books, 2008.

Frederick Taylor, *Dresden*, London, Bloomsbury, 2004.

Peter Barth BSc PhD, was born in Hamburg in 1941. He and his family became refugees in Germany and after the war, moved to Brighton, England. He followed a career as a molecular biologist, studying, teaching and researching in many universities, including Southampton, Leicester, Yale, Kent and the Royal Postgraduate Medical School. His particular interest was the spread of drug-resistant bacteria. He worked in AstraZeneca until retirement. He and his wife now live in a village near Chester.